Erik the Viking

Terry Jones' **Erik the Viking** is a saga of fearless warriors and great adventures on the high seas, of battles fought and won and of women loved and lost. It is a tale of magic, of heroism . . . and of homesickness.

Our hero, Erik the Viking, is a troubled man, a reluctant warrior who has come to believe that life must hold more for him than the daily routine of fighting, raping and pillaging beneath the frozen skies of a never-ending winter.

Setting out to end the age of violence and bring back the sun, he gathers an unlikely and unruly band of followers including Sven the Berserk, Ivar the Boneless, Thorfinn Skull-Splitter and Harald Missionary, who hasn't made a convert in seventeen years. They sail away to awaken the Gods and bring peace to their land, but pursued by the villainous Halfdan the Black who is far from pleased at this threat to the age of violence.

Terry Jones was born in 1942 and was educated at Oxford. His work for television includes *Monty Python's Flying Circus* (1969–74); *Secrets* (written with Michael Palin – 1973); *Ripping Yarns* (also written with Michael Palin – 1977–78). His film work includes *And Now For Something Completely Different* (1970–71); *Monty Python and the Holy Grail* (co-directed with Terry Gilliam, 1975); he also directed *Monty Python's Life of Brian* (1979); *Monty Python's Meaning of Life* (1983); *Personal Services* (1987) and *Erik the Viking* (1989). He is reportedly available for odd jobs, party catering, lunchtime recitals and sells ladies underwear in his spare time.

TERRY JONES

Erik the Viking

The Book of the
Film of the Book

METHUEN DRAMA

A Methuen Screenplay

First published as a paperback original in Great Britain in 1989
by Methuen Drama, Michelin House, 81 Fulham Road, London SW3 6RB.
Copyright © 1989 by Terry Jones

A CIP catalogue record for this book
is available from the British Library.
ISBN 0 413 62680 6

The photographs on the front and back cover and inside the book
are production stills taken by David Appleby, Copyright ©
KB Erik the Viking Film Productions.

Typeset by Hewer Text Composition Services, Edinburgh
Printed and bound in Great Britain by Cox & Wyman Ltd, Reading

Erik the Viking opened in the UK in September 1989

ERIK	Tim Robbins
KEITEL BLACKSMITH	Gary Cady
KING ARNULF	Terry Jones
FREYA	Eartha Kitt
ERIK'S GRANDAD	Mickey Rooney
HALFDAN THE BLACK	John Cleese
SLAVEMASTER	Tsutomu Sekine
LOKI	Antony Sher
IVAR THE BONELESS	John Gordon Sinclair
PRINCESS AUD	Imogen Stubbs
HELGA	Samantha Bond
HARALD MISSIONARY	Freddie Jones
SVEN THE BERSERK	Tim Mcinnerny
SVEN'S DAD-ULF THE MADDENINGLY CALM	Charles McKeown
THORFINN SKULL-SPLITTER	Richard Ridings
SNORRI THE MISERABLE	Danny Schiller

Writer/Director Terry Jones
Producer John Goldstone
Executive Producer Terry Glinwood
Associate Producer Neville C. Thompson
Photographed by Ian Wilson BSC
Production Designer John Beard
Music Neil Innes
Film Editor George Akers
Second Unit Director Julian Doyle
Costume Designer Pam Tait
Special Effects Design Richard Conway
Make-Up and Hair Design Jenny Shircore
Casting Irene Lamb

Filmed on location in Malta, Norway and at Lee International Studios, Shepperton, UK.

A John Goldstone/Prominent Features Production.

Blackness.

Flames begin to lick upwards from the bottom of the screen.

Suddenly all hell breaks loose. Screaming, yelling. Black figures flash across the foreground, with the flames still burning behind.

There follows a confusion of burning, raping, killing and looting – we don't clearly see what's going on.

Suddenly we cut to the interior of a hut. The door is in the process of being broken down. The camera pans onto the close-up face of an attractive girl who is staring in horrified fascination at the door. Her arms are white with fresh dough and flour.

Suddenly the door bursts open and a wild-looking Viking leaps into the hut. He holds a sword. He looks around wildly and then his eyes come to rest on the girl.

This Viking, I'm afraid, is Erik. We are about to see him in the worst possible light so be prepared.

The girl, whose name is Helga, cowers, and looks terrified but resolute.

Erik glances round.

Then slowly he advances on the girl, forcing her back onto a chest.

Erik holds his sword to Helga's throat with his right hand, while his left hand searches to find the thongs holding up his trousers.

He is clearly having difficulty trying to hold his heavy sword to Helga's throat at the same time as undoing his trousers. He fumbles and lowers his sword for a moment.

HELGA. Have you done this sort of thing before?

ERIK. Me? Of course! I've been looting and pillaging up and down the coast.

HELGA (*looking sceptical*). Looting and pillaging, eh?

ERIK (*on the defensive*). Yes.

HELGA. What about the raping?

ERIK. Shut up.

HELGA. It's obvious you haven't raped anyone in your life.
ERIK. Sh!

He covers her mouth with his free hand, and looks round to make sure no one's heard. Then he carries on trying to undo his trousers, but he is now somewhat more than half-hearted about it.

Helga watches suspiciously.

HELGA. Do you *like* women?

Erik is clearly shocked and stung by the insinuation. He stops.

ERIK. Of course I like women . . . I *love* 'em.
HELGA (*pointing out the obvious*). You don't love *me*.
ERIK. No . . . right . . . this is *rape* . . . Mark you, I'm not saying I couldn't get to like you . . . in fact . . . well, to be quite honest, I prefer it when there's some sort of mutual feeling between two people . . .
HELGA. What – rape?
ERIK. No. It isn't rape then, is it?
HELGA. Oh, get it over with.
ERIK (*hesitates again*). I don't suppose . . . no . . .
HELGA. What?
ERIK. I don't suppose you . . . you *do* like me at all?
HELGA. What d'you expect? You come in here, burn my village, kill my family and try to rape me . . .

This is too much for Erik. He withers under the irony.

ERIK. I'll kill you if you say anything about this to anyone.
HELGA (*puzzled*). About raping me?
ERIK. About *not* raping you . . .
HELGA. You *don't* like it, do you?
ERIK. Well it just seems a little bit crude, that's all.
HELGA. What about the killing and looting? That's just as crude, isn't it?
ERIK. Oh well – you've *got* to do them.
HELGA. Why? Why have you got to go round killing and looting?

ERIK. To pay for the next expedition, of course.

HELGA. But that's a circular argument! If the only reason for going on an expedition is the killing and looting and the only reason for the killing and looting is to pay for the next expedition, they cancel each other out.

ERIK. Oh! Stop talking as if we were married!

HELGA. Well you started it.

ERIK. I just said I didn't feel like raping you.

HELGA. And *I* was just saying that rape is no *more* pointless or crude than all the killing and looting that goes on.

Erik vents some of his frustration on the already shattered door.

ERIK. Scream.

HELGA. Ah.

ERIK. Louder.

HELGA. Aaagh! Rape!

ERIK (*he'd forgotten about that*). Oh, thanks.

Two more Vikings burst in with eager eyes blazing. They have the very unfortunate names of Ernest and Jennifer, but it doesn't really matter, for reasons which will become obvious very quickly. They are also slightly drunk.

ERNEST THE VIKING. Rape?

JENNIFER THE VIKING. Where?

Jennifer the Viking sways and leans against a door post. The marauders' eyes come to rest on Erik and Helga who are standing, fully clothed, about six feet apart. They look slightly puzzled.

HELGA. He raped me standing up.

There is a pause. Erik looks up at Helga. Why has she saved his face by telling this lie? Jennifer the Viking turns to Erik.

JENNIFER. You finished, then?

ERIK. Oh . . . yes . . . I suppose so . . .

ERNEST. Right! Me first!

JENNIFER. No! I asked!

Ernest leaps on top of Helga and pins her to the ground.
Jennifer joins in.
Erik looks stunned for a moment. Then he suddenly leaps to
Helga's defence.

ERIK. Leave her alone!

He pulls Jennifer off, but Jennifer fights back. Erik forces
Jennifer back until he falls into the kneading trough. They fight
in the dough for some moments, until Erik runs Jennifer
through. The dough is stained red, and the film is rid of such an
inappropriately named Viking once and for all.
Erik then turns his attention on Ernest who is still on top of
Helga. Without a moment's hesitation, Erik runs him through
the back. Ernest screams. So does Helga. Erik turns white,
and pulls out his sword.
Ernest falls over into a heap with his co-misnomer, and Erik
kneels beside Helga to find a bloodstain under her breast where
he has inadvertently run her through. She is clearly not long for
this world.

HELGA. Thanks for saving me from a fate worse than death.
ERIK. I didn't mean to!
HELGA (*gasping for breath*). Oh, that's all right then . . . it's
the thought . . . that counts . . .

Erik cradles her head and tries helplessly to staunch the blood.

ERIK. You told them I raped you – why?
HELGA (*dying*). I dunno . . . you looked so . . . so vul-
nerable . . .
ERIK. Why should you care?
HELGA (*dying*). Why . . . should *you* care?
ERIK. Tell me your name?

Helga looks up at him, but dies in his arms, without ever saying
her name.

ERIK. Tell me . . . what *is* it . . . ?

Erik realizes she has gone. He gazes at her for some time. He
looks around at the two dead bodies beside them. Then he

listens to the sounds of raping and slaughter continuing on the outside. Screams and bloodthirsty shouts echo alongside the roar of flames and the cries of animals. The camera tracks in to a big close-up on Erik. Superimpose the title: ERIK THE VIKING:

Second title: TIM ROBBINS.

Mix through to wide shot of the burning village. Figures running here and there.
Superimpose the rest of the opening titles.
By the last of the opening titles the last of the flames are dying down.

Cut to a big close-up of a very tough-looking Viking screaming into the camera, as he hurls an axe. This Viking's name is Thorfinn Skull-Splitter.
The axe thuds into the wall a few inches away from the face of a frightened girl, Unn, who is pinned to the wall with her braids spread out. The Vikings are hurling axes at her à la Kirk Douglas in The Vikings.
Several Vikings, sitting at the ale-bench, laugh in a rather unpleasant way.
Erik, however, frowns. He is sitting at a table on a dais, next to his grandfather, the chief of the village. His grandfather almost chokes with merriment. Erik's mother glances at him with some hostility.
Meanwhile the drunken Thorfinn has just lifted the totally legless Ivar the Boneless up off the floor and pressed an axe into his hand. A tremor of nervousness ripples round the females in the Mead Hall. Ivar is clearly in no condition to throw anything, except, perhaps, the contents of his stomach.
Unn winces.
Finally, amidst much giggling, Ivar throws wildly, and the axe smashes into a jug being carried by one of the serving girls.
The menfolk erupt into drunken hysterics at this. The women clearly feel that the occasion is getting out of hand. But before any of them can work up enough courage to intervene, Thorfinn Skull-Splitter has thrust an axe into the hands of the even more

plastered Sven the Berserk. Now Sven is not the Viking to let a little matter like not being able to see straight stop him heaving the axe at a young maiden. He takes the axe and whirls it wildly over his head. Even the other drunken Vikings realize this could be dangerous, and they cower behind the table. Sven lets go of the axe. Unn shuts her eyes prepared for the worst. There is a dull thud and a grunt and then a whoop of mirth. Unn opens her eyes to find that the axe has come to rest in the back of a totally stupefied Viking who merely slumps forward onto the table he is sitting at. On the opposite side sits Harald Missionary, a rather seedy cleric who has long since given up trying to convert the pagans and found solace in their mead. He thinks about intervening, but decides that it's a bit late really and that he might as well finish off his ale-cup instead. Grimhild Housewife (his only admirer) refills it for him.

At this moment, however, the axe-throwers have run out of axes, so, as they go to retrieve the ones they've thrown, Harald Missionary salves his conscience by lurching across to the unfortunate Unn.

He pokes his dog-eared bible under her nose.

HARALD. If you were thinking of converting, my dear, this would be an *ideal* opportunity . . .

UNN. Not now!

HARALD (*who is used to rebuffs*). No, of course not . . . (*He hesitates.*) You might not get another chance, you know . . .

UNN. Go away.

At this moment another axe thuds into the wall, speeding up Harald's desire to get back to the ale-bench.

HARALD. Yes, of course . . . I'll pray for you anyway, my dear . . .

Suddenly an axe shatters a large earthenware vessel.

HARALD. Yes . . . That's what I'll do . . .

Harald scuttles back to the ale-bench as fast as he can.

Erik, meanwhile, stares in astonishment as, for a fleeting moment, he sees Helga, the girl he accidentally killed, standing there with her braids spread out in place of Unn. He shakes his head and the vision passes.

In the meantime, however, Ivar's mum (perhaps the toughest lady in the village) has decided that enough is enough.

IVAR'S MUM. Let her go!

THORFINN. Why?

VIKINGS. Yes, why?

SVEN THE BERSERK. Why should we let her go?

THORFINN SKULL-SPLITTER. We haven't hit a single braid yet!

The Vikings all guffaw.

Ivar's mum has had enough. She throws the contents of a jug of ale over Thorfinn. He is soaked, but after the first shock he grins evilly, because now he's been given carte blanche *to do the thing he enjoys doing most. Without another thought he throws a vicious right hook at Ivar's mum and lays her out cold.*

Erik reacts with disgust.

His grandad, however, gives a whoop of glee.

GRANDAD. Whoah! Heee! That showed her!

Meanwhile a little shrivelled old man is jumping up and down.

INGEMUND THE OLD. Hey! He hit my wife!

Ingemund starts to go for Thorfinn, but Thorhild beats him to it. She grabs one of the long-handled cooking griddles from the fires and swings it at Thorfinn.

Thorfinn, however, ducks, and the red-hot griddle hits Sven the Berserk, who is standing with his back to Thorfinn.

Sven screams and goes berserk, turning round and hitting Thorfinn who is now standing upright again.

INGEMUND THE OLD. Leave him alone.

Ingemund hits Sven. Thangbrand hits Ingemund and a general fight breaks out.

Erik's grandad clearly considers this the highlight of the evening, but Erik looks at it in disgust and at his grandad in despair. Eventually he gets up and walks out of the Mead Hall.

His grandad notices and frowns. He knows something's wrong with his grandson but hasn't a clue what it could be. Erik's mother frowns and nods to his grandad.

Grandad gets up and fights his way through the mêlée to follow Erik out of the Hall.

The snow lies thick over the village as Erik's grandfather joins his grandson beside the little quay. Erik is staring broodily into the night.

GRANDAD. What's the matter, son?

Erik doesn't reply. His grandfather glances back at the Mead Hall, whence the sounds of the fight drift across the snow.

GRANDAD. We're missing all the fun . . .

ERIK. What's it all about?

GRANDFATHER. What?

ERIK. We toil and labour, we loot and pillage, rape and kill . . . and yet . . .

GRANDFATHER. You talking piffle, son?

ERIK. Where does it all get us, Grandpa?

GRANDFATHER. Who have you been talking to?

ERIK. I met this girl . . .

GRANDFATHER. It's always the women that start the trouble.

ERIK. She got me thinking . . .

GRANDFATHER. So? What'd you do to her?

Erik stops in his tracks – as if brought up short by the horror of what he has done.

ERIK. I . . . I . . . *killed* her . . .

GRANDFATHER. That's my boy!

Erik's grandfather gives him a paternal hug. Erik looks at him and thinks about the generation gap.

Cut to feet running through snow. It is day.

ERIK. Freya!

Erik looks around him and calls out again.

ERIK. Freya!

Erik runs into the distance – a small figure against the dramatic wintry landscape.

Cut to a remote, barren mountainside.
Erik climbs up into shot, and continues climbing until he reaches a cave. He enters it. As his eyes get used to the dark he can make out a few signs of life: a cooking pot on a fire, a straw bed, a pile of rune-sticks.

ERIK. Freya? Freya?

There is a bundle of rags behind Erik. A head rises from it. This is Freya.

FREYA. Ah . . . Erik . . . Erik the 'Viking' . . .

It is not clear whether her words are not a little mocking.

FREYA. Now what *can* you want with me, Erik the 'Viking'?
ERIK. I shouldn't have come.
FREYA. They will make fun of you for listening to an old woman's stories?

Erik doesn't reply. Freya watches him craftily.

FREYA. Young men are only interested in fighting and killing.

Erik looks up at her sharply. It is as if she has read his mind.

ERIK. But has it always been like that, Freya? From the beginning of time?

Freya doesn't reply. Instead she walks to the mouth of the cave. Erik follows her. They look out at the grey, desolate landscape. Nothing but arctic wastes, snow and desolation. Above them the black clouds boil ceaselessly.

FREYA. What do you see, Erik?

ERIK. I see the world.

FREYA. Is it night or day, Erik?

ERIK. It is day, of course, Freya.

FREYA. Is it summer or winter, Erik?

Erik looks round at the snowy wastes and then back at Freya, puzzled.

ERIK. The winter is past, thank goodness, Freya. It is summer.

Freya puts her face close to Erik's and peers into his eyes.

FREYA. Have you ever seen the sun, Erik?

ERIK. The sun is up beyond the clouds – where it always is.

FREYA. But have you ever seen it? Think back . . .

ERIK. Of course not . . . but . . . when I was a child . . . I remember a dream . . . it was as if the whole sky were blue . . .

FREYA. The sky *was* blue, Erik . . . once.

Erik looks at her.

FREYA. The Old Stories tell of an age that would come such as this – when Fenrir the Wolf would swallow the sun, and a Great Winter would settle upon the world. It was to be an axe age, a sword age, a storm age, when brother would turn against brother, and men would fight each other until the world would finally be destroyed.

Erik looks out across the bleak and gloomy landscape and the black, boiling clouds in the sky.

ERIK (*almost to himself*). Then . . . this is the Age of Ragnarok?

Freya turns to go back into the cave.

ERIK. Wait, Freya!

Erik re-enters the cave.

ERIK. Is there nothing men can do?

FREYA. The Gods are asleep, Erik.

ERIK. I will go and wake them up!

Freya turns and looks at him. She clearly enjoys his earnest enthusiasm, but is afraid he doesn't know what he is talking about.

ERIK. Tell me what I must do, Freya!

Freya thinks for some moments. Then she speaks.

FREYA. Erik . . . Far out in the midst of the Western Ocean there is a land . . . men call it Hy-Brasil. There you will find a horn that is called Resounding. You must take the Horn Resounding, and three times you must blow it. The first note will take you to Asgaard. The second will awaken the Gods, and the third note will bring you home. But remember . . . once you are in the spell of the Horn, hatred will destroy you.

Erik turns to go and then hesitates.

ERIK. And will the dead ever return, Freya?

FREYA. That I cannot tell you.

Cut to a big close-up of a head being banged on the ground. It is Thorfinn Skull-Splitter's. The person doing the banging is an enraged Sven the Berserk.

Suddenly Erik pushes his way through the crowd and separates them.

There is general disgruntlement all round, and murmurs of: 'Who does he think he is?'

ERIK'S GRANDAD. What are you doing, Erik? Thorfinn just said Sven's grandfather died of old age.

INGEMUND THE OLD. They must fight to the death.

THORFINN SKULL-SPLITTER. That's right! Sven must kill me.

OTHERS. Yes. Stay out of this. What's it to do with you? (etc.)

Sven grinds his teeth and struggles to get at Thorfinn, but Erik still keeps them apart.

ERIK. Aren't you afraid of death, Thorfinn Skull-Splitter?

Thorfinn shrugs.

THORFINN. Not death by the sword! It means I shall drink in Valhalla with the great warriors.

Cut away to Harald Missionary engaged in his usual business of chatting up any available female.

HARALD MISSIONARY. You don't still believe in all that Valhalla stuff, do you?
THORHILD THE FEMALE. Go away.
HARALD. Fine . . . right . . . just checking.

He moves off.

ERIK. And you, Sven, aren't you afraid of crossing the Rainbow Bridge to Asgaard?
SVEN. I will join my grandfather there.
THORFINN. He's not in Valhalla! He died of old age!
SVEN. You liar!

They start trying to kill each other again, and crash through a fence into the pig-sty. Pigs squeal and run in all directions.

ERIK. Stop it!
OTHERS. Leave them alone! Keep out of it, Erik!

The others pull Erik away.

GRANDAD. There's only one way to settle it.
EVERYONE. Yes!
THORFINN. He *must* kill me!
EVERYONE. Yes! That's right! (etc.)

Sven struggles again to oblige, and they both topple into the duck pond. Erik dives back to keep them apart.

ERIK. There is another way.

GRANDAD. Who gets killed?

ERIK. Nobody gets killed.

THORFINN. Oh, well . . .

He starts attacking Sven again. Erik decides there is only one way to make his point. He lets fly with his fists and lays both the antagonists out for a moment.

ERIK. But it will be dangerous. Maybe none of us will return.

SNORRI THE MISERABLE. Ah well, that's much more sensible than just Thorfinn getting killed. Shall we all go and pack now?

SVEN. What are you talking about, Erik?

ERIK. What if we could find Bi-Frost the Rainbow Bridge?

This causes a sensation amongst everyone watching, on the lines of 'You can't do that' and so on. They scoff at Erik.

THORFINN (*in disbelief*). *Find* the Rainbow Bridge?

ERIK. Find it . . . *and* cross it!

Super-sensation amongst everyone – except for Harald Missionary who shakes his head sadly.

HARALD. Look! You can't find somewhere that doesn't exist.

GRANDAD (*to Harald*). Shut up!

Harald shrugs.

SVEN. Only the dead reach Asgaard, Erik.

ERIK. What's the matter? Are you afraid to try?

Thorfinn and Sven are put on the defensive.

THORFINN. Of course we're not afraid to try, but . . .

Erik rounds on Thorfinn, sensing he had the advantage.

ERIK. 'But' what?

THORFINN. But . . .

ERIK. What?

Thorfinn's mental powers find it hard to articulate any proposition on such a vast metaphysical concept. Sven comes to his rescue.

SVEN. Nobody's ever crossed the Rainbow Bridge to Asgaard.

ERIK. We'd be the first!

SNORRI. You mean we'd be dead?

ERIK. No! We'd be the first living men to set foot in the Halls of the Gods.

Pause. Uncomfortable shifting.

SVEN. But *how*?

ERIK. I don't know – but I'm not afraid to try.

THORFINN. Well I'm certainly not, either.

SVEN. Neither am I.

ERIK. Then you'll come.

HARALD. But there isn't such a place as . . . Look . . .

THORFINN AND SVEN. Shut up.

ERIK. What d'you say?

SVEN. Well . . . I'm game.

THORFINN. Me too.

Erik grins. He has persuaded them against their will.

GRANDAD. Aren't you going to go on fighting?

SVEN AND THORFINN. No.

OTHERS. Oh . . .

There is general disappointment all round.

IVAR THE BONELESS. Oh, go on . . .

GRANDAD. Just have a bit of a fight.

INGEMUND THE OLD. *I'll* fight someone.

GRANDAD. You're too old.

INGEMUND THE OLD. No, I ain't.

Cut to an adze striking timber. The Vikings' ship, Golden Dragon, *is being repaired and fitted out for a journey. Erik is there, directing operations.*

The camera tracks through all the activity and finally comes to rest on Keitel Blacksmith. He is a magnificent mountain of a man in an Arnold Schwarzeneggarish sort of way. He hammers a sword, and sparks fly, but his eyes keep returning to the preparations for the voyage. Clearly something is worrying him.

His assistant, Loki, sidles up to him.

LOKI. Wish you were going too?

Keitel grunts angrily and plunges the sword into cold water. Steam and bubbles.

LOKI. But you *can't* because you're too busy.

Keitel pulls the sword out of the water and tests it. It slices like a razor. Loki watches.

LOKI. Ooh, that's a good one! You could charge Halfdan fifteen for that one.

KEITEL. Yes, it is good. But I told him ten.

LOKI. You could charge him what you like.

Loki takes the sword from Keitel and stacks it alongside a lot more freshly made swords.

LOKI. You just can't make enough swords and spears and knives and daggers to satisfy the demand. You could charge Halfdan twenty and he'd pay it.

KEITEL (*shocked*). Oh, I couldn't do that! The Blacksmith's Code says . . .

LOKI. Yes yes . . . of course . . . the 'Blacksmith's Code' . . .

Keitel goes back to his forge and pulls out a fresh dollop of white-hot ore. Loki comes up behind him.

LOKI. If this *is* the Age of Ragnarok, Keitel Blacksmith, it is *good* to us.

KEITEL (*banging with his hammer*). Can't make enough swords!

Bang! Bang! Bang!

KEITEL. Can't make enough axe-heads!

Bang! Bang! Bang!

LOKI. But, Keitel, if Erik ever finds the Horn Resounding . . . if he ever crosses Bi-Frost, the Rainbow Bridge . . . if he ever wakens the gods . . .

Keitel stops smiting the metal on his forge. He stares into space.

KEITEL. They chase Fenrir the Wolf from the sky . . .

LOKI. The Age of Ragnarok ends . . .

KEITEL. The bottom falls out of the sword business!

LOKI. It's not just *your* livelihood that's at stake but your son's, and the livelihood of *all* blacksmiths.

KEITEL (*this touches a nerve in his muscular mind*). My brother blacksmiths!

LOKI. That's right.

KEITEL. The Blacksmith's Code says I must . . .

LOKI. Honour and protect all blacksmiths.

KEITEL (*as if reciting his oath*). Together we stand!

LOKI. You can't let Erik do *that*.

Loki smiles. He has Keitel playing into his hands, although Keitel doesn't realize it.

Fade.

Cut to some days later. The expedition is set to leave. Thorfinn Skull-Splitter taking leave of his mum and dad.

THORFINN'S MUM. And you've got *both* axes?

THORFINN. Yes, Mother.

THORFINN'S MUM. And something to sharpen them with?

THORFINN. Yes, Mum.

THORFINN'S MUM. And don't forget: never let your enemy get behind you.

THORFINN. No, Mother.

THORFINN'S MUM. And keep your sword greased.

THORFINN. Yes, Mother. Goodbye, Dad.

THORFINN'S DAD. And don't forget to wash – you know – *all* over.

THORFINN. No, Dad.

THORFINN'S MUM. And if you have to kill somebody, *kill* them! Don't stop to think about it.

THORFINN (*mildly*). I never do . . .

Cut to Sven the Berserk who is also being lectured. The lecture is coming from his father – Ulf the Maddeningly Calm.

SVEN'S FATHER (*sotto voce*). It's a tradition.

SVEN. I know, Dad.

SVEN'S FATHER. I was a Berserk for King Harald Fairhair . . .

SVEN. You went berserk . . .

SVEN'S FATHER. I went berserk in every battle I ever fought for King Harald . . .

SVEN. So did your father . . .

SVEN'S FATHER. So did my father and his father before him.

SVEN. But it's a responsibility . . .

SVEN'S FATHER. But it's a responsibility being a Berserk.

SVEN. I must only let the red rage . . .

SVEN'S FATHER. You must only let the red rage take hold of you in the thick of battle.

SVEN (*losing his temper*). I KNOW! I'VE HEARD IT ALL A THOUSAND TIMES!

A sudden silence falls, as all the village turns to stare nervously at Sven. He goes berserk and demolishes a nearby hut with his head. Ulf the Maddeningly Calm shakes his head.

SVEN'S FATHER. No no . . . you'll never make a Berserk. If you let it out now you'll have nothing left for battle . . .

IVAR'S MUM. Besides . . . it's dangerous.

SVEN'S FATHER (*gloomily*). It's the end of a family tradition.

In another corner of the village Leif the Lucky is standing with his pregnant girlfriend.

GIRL. Bye, Leif.

LEIF. Bye . . . sorry . . .

GIRL. Yeah . . . well . . .

LEIF. You will wait?

GIRL. What d'you expect me to do?

She takes a bracelet off her arm and gives it to Leif.

GIRL. Wear this for luck.

Leif looks at it.

LEIF. That's what they call me . . . Leif the Lucky.
GIRL. Please.

Cut to Harald Missionary dumping a bag on board the ship. Grimhild Housewife is helping him.
    Snorri looks at him in surprise.

SNORRI. *You* coming? You don't even believe in Asgaard.
HARALD. I thought I might do a bit of business on the way.
SNORRI. You're wasting your time.
HARALD. Listen. I've been in this dump for sixteen years and I haven't made a single convert . . .
SNORRI. There was Thorbjorn Vifilsson's wife. You converted *her*.
HARALD. Thorbjorn Vifilsson's wife became a Buddhist, not a Christian.
SNORRI. Same thing, isn't it?
HARALD. No, it is *not*.

Meanwhile in another part of the village, Loki is strapping a large consignment of swords onto a pony. He glances round and then sneaks surreptitiously out of the village, over the barren hills of Norway, under the boiling black skies of Ragnarok.

Back at the quayside, Golden Dragon is ready for the journey.
    Erik addresses the villagers.

ERIK. Well . . . we'll be off now . . .

Erik's grandad waits for some time before he realizes that Erik isn't intending to say anything else.
GRANDAD. You need to say a bit more than that!
ERIK. Oh . . . er . . . yes . . .

The faces of the village-folk turn towards him. There are many moist eyes. Erik's mother starts to cry.

ERIK. Oh, there, Mum . . . (*He turns and addresses everyone.*) Don't be sad . . . You all know why we're going, so don't grieve. Maybe untold dangers do lie ahead of us, and some of you may well be looking at the one you love for the last time . . .

Someone bursts out sobbing. Erik desperately tries to rally their spirits.

ERIK. But don't grieve! Even though the Hordes of Muspel tear us limb from limb . . . or the Fire Giants burn each and every one of us to a cinder . . .

More crying.

ERIK. . . . though we may be swallowed by the Dragon of the North Sea or fall off the Edge of the World . . . don't cry.

More crying.

ERIK. No! *Don't* cry . . .

By this time most of the village is blubbering profusely.

Cut to Harald Missionary. He has his arm round his weeping girlfriend.

HARALD MISSIONARY. Sh . . . There . . . it's all fantasy, there's no Dragon of the North Sea, no Edge of the World . . .

GRIMHILD HOUSEWIFE. That's what *you* say.

ERIK (*aside to his grandad*). What's the matter with them?

GRANDAD. Just say something cheerful.

ERIK. Oh . . . right! (*He can't think of anything.*) Well . . . CHEERS everybody!

Erik smiles broadly and waves. The entire village stares back at him with tears in their eyes, and biting their lips. Suddenly one mother can't hold it back any more.

THORFINN'S MUM. Don't go!

Another mother rushes out and grabs Ivar the Boneless.

IVAR'S MUM. My son! I don't want you to go!

IVAR. I don't want to go, either . . .

ERIK. Oh gods! Please, everybody! Keep calm! It's not certain *all* of us are going to die . . . and in any case we may not die *hideous* deaths . . .

More renewed sobbing. Grandad's eyes go heavenwards.

GRANDAD (*to Erik*). I think we should go . . .

ERIK. Right. (*He turns for a last salute.*) Farewell . . . for the last time . . . may the gods prevent . . .

GRANDAD. No, don't say anything else!

Suddenly Keitel the Blacksmith steps forward. His muscles ripple. His handsome face radiates heroism and manliness.

KEITEL. Wait, Erik!

ERIK. Keitel Blacksmith?

They stop and turn.

KEITEL. You can't go without me. Who will repair your swords and mend your shields?

Renewed sobs from the women.

WOMEN. Oh, no! Ah, lackaday! Not *him* too!

ERIK. What's the matter *now*?

UNN. If Keitel Blacksmith goes with you . . .

THORHILD. We'll have no one to do the things he did for us.

THORKATLA THE INDISCREET. *Or* sharpen our knives and make our pans.

An awkward silence. The others all turn on her and frown – a bit of shin-kicking goes on. It's clear that Keitel is popular amongst the womenfolk. Erik doesn't notice.

ERIK. You will have Keitel's assistant, Loki, to do all that.

WOMEN. Loki? Eurrgh!

ERIK. What's wrong with Loki? He's become very good at blacksmithing.

WOMEN. Yes . . . but . . .

THORKATLA. He's so small and . . .

The others all shush her up. More shin-kicking.

THORHILD (*innocently*). Oh, yes . . . we've got Loki . . .
That's true . . .

*Cut to Loki leading his pony across a bleak landscape. He
eventually stops and looks ahead. There stands a gibbet with two
corpses dangling from it. He is nearing his destination.*

Cut back to Erik and his men getting into Golden Dragon.

*Erik notices Thorfinn and Sven quarrelling over Leif the
Lucky.*

ERIK. Hey, you two! What's going on?
SVEN. I was sitting there.
LEIF. No, you weren't.
THORFINN. Leif's sitting here. I need a bit of luck.
LEIF. See.
SVEN. Look, I bagged it last week.
ERIK. It doesn't matter *where* you sit!
SVEN. Yes it does! We could be at sea for months.
ERIK. Well, what difference does it make where you're
sitting?
SVEN. I don't want to have to sit next to Snorri all that time.

*Sven nods towards Snorri the Miserable – an Eeyore of a
Viking if ever there were one.*

SNORRI. Thank you *very* much indeed.
ERIK. Now stop it!
SNORRI. It's *so* nice to feel wanted.
ERIK. Leif, you sit there. Sven, you sit there. Harald, you'd
better sit over there . . .
SNORRI. Trust me to get the missionary.

Suddenly Erik notices Sven's father climbing aboard.

ERIK. What are *you* doing here?

SVEN'S DAD. You may need a real Berserk.

SVEN. I *am* one, Dad!

ERIK. We haven't got a spare place.

IVAR. He can have my place. I don't want to go anyway.

ERIK. Well, you *are*!

KEITEL. Bjorn's not. He could have Bjorn's place.

ERIK. What's the matter with Bjorn?

THORFINN. Nothing . . . Halfdan the Black chopped his hand off last night.

ERIK. *He* was lucky . . . (*To Sven's dad.*) Sit there.

SNORRI. You can't have Sven's father sitting next to Sven. They'll argue the whole time.

ERIK. That's true. (*To Sven.*) *You'd* better sit there. (*To Sven's dad.*) You there, and Ornulf there.

SNORRI. Now you've got all the big ones on one side.

Erik looks around. It is true that all the tall burly ones are on one side.

ERIK. All right, you go there. You here . . .

Sven's dad and Ornulf swap places.

SVEN'S DAD. Ohh! I wanted to sit next to Leif.

ERIK. Shut up. You there. You there and you there.

Ivar and Ornulf swap places.
Erik surveys this re-arrangement.

ERIK. That's better.

SNORRI. Now you've got all the ones with beards on one side and all the moustaches on the other.

This is true. Erik thinks for some moments and then:

ERIK. It doesn't matter.

They start to haul the sail up. Ropes are released. The boat rocks.
Suddenly a voice cuts through the crowd. It is Erik's mother.

ERIK'S MUM. Wait! Wait! Wait!

ERIK. What is it? (*He is clearly a little embarrassed.*)

ERIK'S MUM. Here, son.

*She tries to hand Erik what looks unmistakably like a pillow.
Erik is dumbfounded.*

ERIK'S MUM. Your father always made sure he could rest his
head at night.

*Erik is mortified. The others snigger, though not without some
sympathy for Erik. They've all been embarrassed by their
mums at one time or another.*

ERIK. I can't take *that* on a voyage!

ERIK'S MUM. It was your father's!

Erik will find it hard to refuse now. But he hesitates.

ERIK'S MUM. It was the pillow *he* took with him. He said it
once saved his life.

*Erik reluctantly takes the precious object. His mother kisses
him.*

*Everyone has fallen silent now. The relatives stand helpless on
the shore as* Golden Dragon *starts to drift away from them.
The Vikings sit in their places, hands on the oars, looking back
at their loved ones.*

Erik stands at the prow of Golden Dragon. *For a moment he
thinks he sees the girl he killed, standing, white in death, the
spear-wound still fresh. Erik raises his hand in a half-goodbye.*

*We cut back to the loved ones, now the girl is no longer there. They
too half-raise their hands.*

Erik suddenly turns and gives a shout:

ERIK. Huuup!

The oars go up and then into the water, and Golden Dragon
commences her voyage.

*Cut to a skull crawling with maggots. It is hanging on a gate at
which Loki is now knocking politely. A grim guard opens the
gate.*

GUARD. What is your business?

LOKI (*a trifle nervous*). I wish to speak to Halfdan the Black.

GUARD. He's too busy.

LOKI. I have money! See!

> *He holds out a gold coin. The guard grabs it and nods Loki into the castle.*

Within the courtyard is a dismal sight. Wretched men and women are being tortured. Some are tied up on frames and are being flayed with whips. Others are tied to posts, apparently awaiting ordeal by fire.

There is a pile of dead bodies at one end of the courtyard. As Loki is hustled towards the main hall, he just glimpses some strange figures who emerge from the smoke of a pyre to fling some more dead bodies on the pile. The figures are almost surreal . . . huge creatures with a man's body and a dog's head. Loki draws his breath in but has no time to look more closely, as he is pushed into the main Hall.

Cut to Halfdan the Black.

> *He is a surprisingly amiable character. Before him a wretched farmer, Thord Andresson, is pinioned by two guards. His wife and children are being held behind him.*

HALFDAN. Look, I'm not an unreasonable man, Thord Andresson, but this is the *second* chance I've given you . . .

THORD ANDRESSON. But I'm a poor man.

HALFDAN. It's not just me – a lot of people depend on this money. I really *can't* give you a third chance . . .

> *Halfdan nods and the wretched farmer is hustled away. His wife and children scream.*

THORD (*yelling*). Take *all* my sheep!

HALFDAN (*with a charming smile*). I shall. Thank you . . .

WIFE. No! No! Thord!

CHILDREN. Daddy!

They are all hustled past. Halfdan shakes his head sadly.

HALFDAN. If only they'd think ahead. I *wish* they would.

The guard marches Loki up to Halfdan's throne.

HALFDAN. Ah! The blacksmith's assistant from Ravens-fjord . . .

As Loki stands before Halfdan, guards keep presenting wretched prisoners to Halfdan.

HALFDAN (*looking a prisoner up and down*). Garrotting.

Halfdan nods and Prisoner 1 is hustled off.

PRISONER I. But lord —

Prisoners 2 and 3 are brought forward by Guard 2.

LOKI. My lord, Halfdan the Black.
HALFDAN. You've brought me more swords?
LOKI. I bring more than swords. I bring a warning from my master.
HALFDAN. A warning? (*Turning to the two prisoners.*) Flay them alive.
PRISONERS 2 and 3. No! Listen! Please! It's all a mistake! I can pay tomorrow! No! Help!

They are dragged off.

LOKI. Erik and the men of Ravensfjord are setting off to cross the Western Ocean.
HALFDAN. Lucky things! *I* could do with a holiday, I can tell you . . . all this financial work gives me a headache . . .

He turns to examine a prisoner who has been literally tied into a knot and is now suspended from a pole.

HALFDAN. Flayed alive, garrotted and *then* beheaded.
KNOTTED PRISONER. No! NO! NO! I'm *not* Hildir Eysteinsson! I'm Hjalti Skeggjason! You've got the wrong man!

He is carried off.

LOKI (*trying to ignore the prisoner's screams*). They seek to drive Fenrir the Wolf from the sky . . . to wake the Gods and bring the Age of Ragnarok to an end.

Halfdan's advisers, Gisli Oddsson and Eilif the Mongol, suddenly show intense interest.

GISLI ODDSSON. *End* Ragnarok?

EILIF THE MONGOL. Who do they think they are?

HALFDAN (*to Guard 5*). Just cut off his hand.

PRISONER 5. Thank you! Oh thanks, my merciful lord! Thank you a million thankyous. Cut them *both* off if you want . . .

Prisoner 5 is hustled off in a flurry of gratitude.

HALFDAN. And why should *you* tell me this?

LOKI. Because, my lord, my livelihood depends on it . . . Like yours . . .

The advisers glance uneasily at Halfdan, unsure how he will react to this potential insult. Loki himself fears he may have gone too far. But Halfdan smiles condescendingly.

HALFDAN. Besides . . . were anything to happen to your master . . . you would take over as blacksmith at Ravensfjord . . .

Loki smiles. Halfdan and he understand each other perfectly.

Cut back to Golden Dragon *at sea.*
    Snorri is feeling queasy and gazing gloomily at the receding coastline of Norway. Thangbrand is sitting near him and feeling equally queasy.

SNORRI. Have a good look . . . that's the last we'll see of old Norway.

Snorri is desperately trying to control his insides.

SNORRI. Goodbye home . . . Goodbye family . . . Goodbye loved ones . . . (*He starts to throw up.*) Goodbye lunch . . .

THANGBRAND. Oh! Shut up.

Harald Missionary puts his arm around Snorri.

HARALD. You know, my son, our lord said . . .

SNORRI. *Your* lord.

HARALD. Quite . . . *my* lord . . . said: 'The Prayer of Faith shall save the sick.'

SNORRI. I hope the Dragon of the North Sea gets *you and* your lord.

Harald Missionary gives him a condescending smile and a weary shake of the head. He knows the Dragon of the North Sea does not exist.

HARALD. Darkness and ignorance . . .

Meanwhile Ivar the Boneless and Sven the Berserk are both suffering from the effects of the sea.

SVEN (*keeping a wave of nausea down*). It's not so bad when you're rowing.

THORFINN SKULL-SPLITTER. That's right.

Thorfinn gobs onto the whetstone with which he is sharpening his axe. Sven can control himself no longer. He rushes for the side.

SVEN THE BERSERK. I want to die.

This sets off Ivar.

IVAR THE BONELESS. Uh oh!

He leaps up and pukes over the side. Mass puking breaks out all over the boat.
Keitel Blacksmith looks around at his preoccupied shipmates, and it slowly dawns upon him that this might be the moment to try a little sabotage.
He goes to the ship's lodestone, which is hanging from the mast. Keitel glances around. No one is looking, but this sort of covert behaviour goes against his normally sunny and open disposition.

KEITEL (*to himself*). The Blacksmith's Code . . .

He steels himself, takes down the lodestone, snaps out the piece
of metal in the base and throws it over the side.
Keitel hangs it up again on the mast.

Ivar is in the stern leaning over the side, looking very green.
Thorfinn looms up behind him with a malevolent grin. He gives
Ivar a hearty slap on the back, bringing up the little that was left
in Ivar's gut.

THORFINN. You all right?

IVAR. No, I'm not.

THORFINN. You don't need to feel bad about being sea-sick,
you know.

IVAR. How can you help feeling bad when you're sea-sick?

THORFINN. I mean many of the greatest sailors were.

Pause.

IVAR. I know. I know.

THORFINN. Olaf Tryggvason used to throw up on every
single voyage . . . the whole time . . . non-stop . . .
puke . . . puke . . . puke.

IVAR. Look! I don't feel *bad* about it. I just feel *ill*.

Thorfinn pauses and waits for a wave of nausea to creep up on
Ivar.

THORFINN. He used to puke in his sleep.

IVAR. Bastard.

He throws up.
Meanwhile Erik is in the stern, gazing out behind them.

ERIK. Thorfinn . . . look over there.

Thorfinn leaves Ivar and joins Erik.
On the horizon a sinister black sail is following them. Thorfinn
grins with evil pleasure. He scents a fight.
Erik turns to the crew.

ERIK. Break out the oars!

Thorfinn's smile disappears and he spins round to confront Erik.

THORFINN. What are you talking about?
ERIK (*to his reluctant crew*). Come on, move it!

Most of the men are being sea-sick.

MORD FIDDLE. We've only just started cooking lunch.

The crew glance at Mord Fiddle and then turn and throw up again.

ERIK. Move it!

Reluctantly the crew take up their rowing positions.
Thorfinn buttonholes Erik (except of course that he doesn't have any buttonholes).

THORFINN. It's Halfdan the Black!
ERIK. I know. Snorri! Get your oar out!

Snorri is sitting in position but without his oar.
Keitel has meanwhile joined them. He, too, stares at the horizon. He is a little puzzled by this turn of events. Loki has said nothing about Halfdan coming after them.

KEITEL (*uneasily*). Do you suppose he wants to stop us waking the Gods?

Erik looks at Keitel with a certain amount of contempt. Keitel is not renowned even amongst these Vikings for his brain-power.

ERIK. What do you think?
KEITEL. But how could he know . . . unless . . .

Keitel stops in mid-sentence as he realizes it must be Loki's doing.

THORFINN (*scornfully*). So are you going to run away from him, Erik?

Erik turns to Thorfinn.

ERIK. Row, Thorfinn Skull-Splitter.

Thorfinn hesitates.

ERIK. And you, Keitel Blacksmith.
KEITEL. But . . .

*Keitel shrugs and turns to take up his rowing position. He is still a little confused by this turn of events.
Erik confronts Thorfinn.*

ERIK. I gave an order. Or didn't you hear?

There is something about Erik's manner that carries an authority that Thorfinn cannot argue with.

ERIK. Come on, Ivar.

*Erik manhandles Ivar over to his drum and thrusts his drumsticks into his hands.
Halfdan's ship is twice the size of Erik's and, as Erik is only too well aware, consequently travels at twice the speed. There is no real chance of them escaping, unless . . . Erik suddenly catches sight of a thick bank of mist in the distance, and steers his ship towards it.*

IVAR *(still feeling ill)*. I want to die . . . *(Then, suddenly catching sight of Halfdan's ship behind them.)* No, I don't!
ERIK. Row! Row! Row!

*Ivar tries to get into the new rhythm, but has a bit of difficulty.
As Halfdan's ship gains on them inexorably, Golden Dragon glides into the sea mist. There is a tremendous roll of thunder very close. All the Vikings look scared. Erik, however, grins.*

ERIK. Row! Row! Row!

He doubles the speed. The drum beats faster.

SVEN'S DAD *(shouts out angrily)*. We can't keep this up!

Erik grins and then leans on the steering oar. Golden Dragon curves around to its left. Then Erik lays his hand on Ivar's drum and silences it.

ERIK. Oars up!

The Vikings ship their oars and sit there in the mist listening to beating of Halfdan's drum getting closer and closer.

At the final moment, however, Halfdan swings his ship in the opposite direction from Erik's and the sound of his drum disappears into the mist. Erik's men breathe a sigh of relief . . . even Keitel Blacksmith . . .
Fade.

Fade up some time later. Golden Dragon *is still drifting in the mist.*
Erik has his fish-lodestone and is trying the direction, but the lodestone is just swinging round uselessly. After trying a few times, Erik gives up and throws the lodestone away into the boat.
The men peer into the thick mist; they are lost.
Suddenly Erik sees something ahead.

ERIK. The Gates of the World . . .
MORD FIDDLE. What?

Golden Dragon *silently guides between two weird islands.*

ERIK. We have passed through the Gates of the World. (*He looks around at the others.*) Now we are in the Unknown . . .

Golden Dragon *drifts on and the mist gets thicker. There is a crash of thunder. Then a series of flashes lights up the mist around them. The Vikings are uneasy, sensing a storm brewing.*
Suddenly Erik points above them. The others look up too. They all gasp.

ERIK (*hardly daring to breathe*). So *that* is what the sun looks like!

Above them hangs a luminous yellow globe, its light just breaking through the mist.

VIKINGS (*to each other*). The sun! It's the sun! Look!
SVEN'S DAD (*in wonderment*). I never thought I should live to see the sun again.

HARALD MISSIONARY. Where?

The Vikings all gaze up above them in awe. Harald looks from one to the other and then tries to follow their eyelines. He clearly can't see it. Magic music fills the air.
Suddenly the 'sun' swoops off to one side and starts swaying from one side to another.
Erik frowns.

ERIK. Should the sun do that?
HARALD MISSIONARY. What are you looking at?
ERIK. Look out!
VIKINGS. Ah!

The Vikings scream and flatten themselves against the sides of the boat, as the 'sun' suddenly lurches down on them out of the sky, revealing for the first time that it is not *the sun at all but a strange monster with a long neck that disappears off into the mist and a glowing globe for a head, and huge chomping jaws. The Vikings are, understandably, terrified.*

VIKINGS. It's not the sun! It's not the sun!
HARALD MISSIONARY. What is it?
SNORRI. It's the Dragon of the North Sea!
HARALD MISSIONARY (*knowingly*). Ah! *That's* why I can't see it.

As the Dragon of the North Sea rises up again, however, its jaw apparently drops off and falls to the deck, and lands on Snorri.

SNORRI. Aaah!

Keitel nervously picks it up and holds it up for everyone to see. It is a strand of sea-weed. The Vikings are non-plussed. They look back up at their now jawless monster. Harald Missionary picks up the sea-weed.

HARALD. Some dragon! Ooh!

He tosses it back amongst his terrified companions.
Suddenly there is an incredibly loud clap of thunder and flames shoot out of the mist.

SVEN. Look out!

*As . . . unbelievably . . . a huge monstrous visage looms out of
the mist . . . It is a creature from the nethermost depths of the
ocean . . . and the incandescent globe is no more than a
sprouting on the end of its nose! More fire shoots out from its
nostrils and sends all the Vikings (and even Harald Missionary) diving for the deck. Then the monstrous head disappears
back into the mist as quickly as it came, taking its light with
it . . .*
The Vikings are paralysed with fear for one brief moment.

ERIK. Row! ROW!

They all scramble for the oars in a determined hysteria.
*Ivar the drummer, in his panic, has set a ridiculously fast rate
and nobody can keep up with it.*

ERIK. Slower! Nobody can row at that speed!
IVAR (*hoarsely*). Sorry.
HARALD. What's all the panic about?
SVEN'S DAD (*in a panic, shouting back over his shoulder*). The
Dragon . . .

Harald gives a patronising smile.

HARALD. Children afraid of the dark . . .

*Suddenly there is another roar, and flames shoot out of the mist
and across the deck of* Golden Dragon.
*One man, Ornolf Fishdriver, who hasn't had much to say so
far, is set on fire. Another, Bjarni Jerusalem-Farer, who has
and will have even less to say than Ornolf Fishdriver, leaps out
of the way of the flames and falls over the side.*

THORFINN. Man overboard!

Thorfinn starts trying to fish him out.
Ivar has started to panic and is beating the drum too fast.

ERIK. Slower! In . . . Out . . .
IVAR. Sorry!

SVEN (*his eyes showing their whites*). We're being attacked!
KILL! Kill! Kill!

SVEN'S DAD. Not now, Sven . . .

SVEN. I must KILL! Kill!

SVEN'S DAD. It's no good going berserk against a dragon!

Sven's dad slaps him around the face.
There is another roar from the monster. Erik turns to Ivar.

ERIK. Faster!

IVAR Make your mind up.

Suddenly the Dragon's head appears out of the mists above
them once again.
There is panic amongst the Vikings as some start to row faster
than others. Screams.

ERIK. Keep up the strike!

The Dragon's jaws open. Flame licks out, and down the centre
of the vessel. There are screams as the Vikings leap out of the
way.
Sven goes berserk again.

SVEN. KILL! KILL!

SVEN'S DAD. Stop it!

The dragon's eyes dilate and its jaws open.
The men throw themselves to the deck as if expecting more fire.
But instead the creature's fangs crash into the wood of the stern
of Golden Dragon.

ERIK. ROW!

SVEN. DEATH!

SVEN'S DAD. Shut UP!

ERIK. Row!

Erik looks around at his terror-stricken crew. He realizes this is
an important moment. It is up to him to save the situation.
Suddenly an idea occurs to him, as he catches sight of the pillow
that his mother gave him.

ERIK. Keep rowing!

Erik dashes to his sea-chest under the mast and pulls out the pillow.

THORFINN. Erik! Row! What are you doing?
ERIK (*holding up the pillow*). It saved my father!

Erik starts to shin up the mast.

SNORRI. Barmy.

Sven's dad is desperately holding Sven back.

SVEN'S DAD. *Hold* it! *Hold* it in!
SVEN. DEATH TO DRAGONS!
ERIK. Row!
SNORRI. Has anyone told him we've got a dragon eating our boat?

Erik has reached the top of the mast and is now right up with the incandescent globe on the end of the long stalk that grows from the creature's nose. He grabs hold of it and swings across onto the monster's nose.
At this moment Sven breaks free of his dad and throws himself onto one of the dragon's teeth.

SVEN. Red mist!

He bangs his head against the monstrous denture.
Sven's dad looks heavenward in despair.

Cut to Harald Missionary who is offering his bible to the petrified Vikings in the prow.

HARALD. It's at times like this that you'll find this book *most* useful, you know . . .

Keitel takes the bible from him and hits him over the head with it.

KEITEL. Row! You idiot!

The monster's eyes dilate wildly as they try to focus on the tiny figure of Erik on its snout.

Erik shoves the pillow up one of the Dragon's nostrils.
Snorri watches Erik incredulously. He shakes his head.

SNORRI. His father went crazy too . . . Used to take forty winks in the middle of a battle . . .

Thorfinn frowns – he has a glimmering of an idea of what Erik is doing.
Erik now plunges his sword through the pillow in the Dragon's nostril, and feathers immediately fly into the air.

ERIK. Now . . . take a deep breath.

The Dragon goes cross-eyed, trying to see what's going on on its snout.

ERIK. Go on! Breathe in, you cod-brain!

Meanwhile the Dragon's tongue suddenly licks out around its tooth. Sven instantly slices through it with his sword. The bright blood spurts, like bursting a sausage. The Dragon gives an agonized roar and a sharp intake of breath. The feathers that have leaked out from the pillow are instantly sucked inside and the whole pillow disappears right up the Dragon's nose.
For a moment everyone holds their breath.
The Dragon's eyes dilate wildly.
Then it wrinkles its snout.
Then it starts what is unmistakably a sneeze.

THE DRAGON OF THE NORTH SEA. Ah . . . ah . . . ah . . .
ERIK. Hold TIGHT!
THE DRAGON OF THE NORTH SEA. Ah . . . ah . . . ah . . .

Erik leaps back across the mast.

THE DRAGON OF THE NORTH SEA. *CHOO!!*

A hurricane of wind and feathers blasts out of the Dragon's nostrils and hits all the Vikings at once.
Everyone is disgusted by the Dragon's breath.

SNORRI. Urgh! What's it been eating?

But the blast has already catapulted the boat into the sky, and it hurtles through the clouds, leaving the Dragon of the North Sea far behind.
They all look up at Erik and cheer.

Shot of Erik. He doesn't look too happy.

Neither does Ivar the Boneless, because he too has just noticed that they are now flying and the ocean is several thousand feet below them.
Ivar screams. The others all rush to the side to look too.

ERIK. No! No! Get back!

Unfortunately they all rush to the same side and the boat tips over with far more instability than when it is in the water.
Leif and Thangbrand are catapulted down into the sea. We watch them descend into tiny dots and tiny unheard splashes below.

THORFINN. Who was that?
SNORRI. Leif the Lucky.

Others are almost falling out. There is renewed panic.

ERIK. Get back!

Poor Erik is still up the mast but has been dislodged and is now hanging on by his hands, dangling over the open sea.
Some of the men – Thorfinn and Sven the Berserk amongst them – are hauling themselves up the almost vertical slope of the deck, trying to redress the balance. Meanwhile Keitel Black-smith is dangling by one hand.

KEITEL. I can't hold on! I can't hold on!

Sven worms his way along the edge – at great peril to himself – and grabs Keitel's wrist just as his fingers slip.

KEITEL. Aaagh!
SVEN. Got you!

Keitel looks up into Sven's eyes. He is totally at Sven's mercy. What thoughts are going through his mind? How is he going to betray Sven in future if he is rescued? Guilt suddenly overwhelms him.

KEITEL. Let me go, Sven.

SVEN. What are you talking about?

KEITEL. I'm not worth risking your life for.

SVEN. I've got you, Keitel Blacksmith. If you go . . . I go too . . .

KEITEL. For your own sake . . . For the others . . . I . . .

SVEN. Hang on . . .

The boat begins to right itself just as Erik finally can't hold on any more, and he plummets, straight into the ship, and through the bottom up to his waist. His legs dangle.
At the same moment the prow of the boat tips and suddenly they are plummeting down towards the ocean.
They hit the water with an almighty splash. Erik is thrown clear of the hull by the force of the water now cascading up through the hole he has made.

SNORRI. First we're flying – now we're sinking!

ERIK. Well, come on!

He whisks off his helmet and starts bailing. All follow suit. Night falls.

Some time later.
The Vikings are still bailing out, but the water is up to their thighs.

IVAR THE BONELESS. Who are we fooling? It's hopeless!

Ivar flings down the helmet with which he's been bailing. The others look at each other. They are reconciled to the fact that they are going to drown.

HARALD MISSIONARY (*hopelessly*). Let's sing something!

SNORRI. Anyone know any good drowning songs?

The suggestion falls flat.

ERIK. Listen! Maybe we won't get to Hy-Brasil! Maybe we
  won't find the Horn Resounding . . . but at least we've
  tried . . . and at least we shall have died like men.
SNORRI. Like fish.
SVEN. Shut up.
THORFINN (*raising his sword*). Erik's right! We'll all meet in
  Valhalla.
IVAR. I don't want to die!
HARALD MISSIONARY. Isn't there *anybody* who'd like to be
  christened before we go down?

Silence. A distinct lack of enthusiasm.

HARALD. It can't do you any *harm* . . .
SVEN'S DAD. What do we have to do?
HARALD. Nothing . . . I just immerse you in water . . .
THORFINN AND OTHERS. Get lost . . .

*The ship creaks and starts to go under. Erik picks up his sword.
The others follow suit.*

ERIK. Don't let me drown, Thorfinn!

*Water starts to pour over the sides of the boat. Erik and
Thorfinn raise their swords to each other.*

THORFINN. Till we meet in Valhalla.

*They all prepare to run each other through. The boat sinks
rapidly.*

IVAR THE BONELESS. I'm too young! Oh Odin! Not me!
  Please not me! Perhaps I'd rather drown . . .
HARALD MISSIONARY. I do *wish* you'd let me convert you.

*Then Erik pauses in his attempt to kill Thorfinn and looks
around. The ship has sunk, but the prow and the stern posts are
still sticking up out of the water, and the Vikings themselves are
only up to their chests.*

ERIK. How deep *is* the ocean?
THORFINN. Very deep . . . usually . . .

The realization gradually dawns on the Vikings that they're not going to sink any more.

ERIK. Wait! Nobody kill anybody!

Fade.

Fade up on the sun shining down from a blue sky. The Vikings have fallen asleep where we last saw them – up to their necks in water. Gradually the warmth of the sun coaxes them awake – Thorfinn is the first to look up and see the brilliant shining orb in the sky.

THORFINN. What is it?

IVAR THE BONELESS (*he panics and turns*). It's the Dragon again!

ERIK. No . . . no, it isn't . . .

Ivar has turned and is staring at something else.

ERIK. Look, the sky is blue . . .

SVEN'S DAD. The sun! That's it!

Ivar, meanwhile, is recovering from the amazement that has immobilized him. He taps Erik on the shoulder. Erik turns and he, too, gasps.

ERIK. Look!

They all turn to see they are standing in the shallow waters of a natural harbour. Above nestle the white walls of a beautiful city set in a green and pleasant land.

VIKINGS. Yeaaaah!

The Vikings wade ashore, enchanted by the paradise they see before them. All at once Thorfinn spies something. He draws his sword and they all approach with caution to find that under a weeping willow lies the most beautiful girl. She is raven-haired, scantily dressed and fast asleep.

The Vikings approach her with trepidation, their swords and axes drawn. They glance around uneasily.

SNORRI (*whispers*). She's got no clothes on!

THORFINN. It's disgusting.

ERIK. Get her weapons.

Sven kneels quietly beside the girl. She stirs. Sven freezes. The others look round fearfully.

SVEN (*whispers*). She hasn't got any!

ERIK (*incredulous*). She *must* have a knife or something . . .

But they look. She hasn't.

THORFINN. What kind of a place *is* this?

IVAR THE BONELESS. P . . . p . . . perhaps they've got weapons we haven't even dreamed of . . .

Suddenly the girl stirs again in her sleep.
The Vikings retreat several paces and grip their weapons, and glance around as if expecting an ambush.

THORFINN. Let's hack her to pieces.

ERIK. No.

KEITEL. Well, what else do we do?

ERIK. How about making friends?

SVEN (*with disgust*). 'Friends'?

VIKINGS. Eurrgh!

ERIK. What's wrong with making friends?

THORFINN. You don't go through all the hardships of an ocean voyage to make 'friends'.

SVEN. We can make 'friends' at home . . .

This conversation has woken the girl, Aud.

AUD. Welcome!

The Vikings react with terror, take a step back and raise their swords and axes.

ERIK. *What* did you say?

AUD. I said you are welcome.

ERIK (*suspiciously*). *Welcome*?

AUD. Well, of course. We always welcome friends.

The Vikings look at each other and at their swords. They don't think they look that much like friends themselves.

ERIK. How d'you *know* we're 'friends'?
AUD. Well, *everyone* is friends here on Hy-Brasil.
SVEN. Hy-Brasil?
ERIK. Is *this* Hy-Brasil?
AUD. Well, of course.

The Vikings erupt into an impromptu dance of joy, hugging each other and waving their swords in the air.

AUD. Please! Please! What are those?
ERIK. What are what?
AUD. Those things in your hands.
ERIK. These? What are *these*? They're swords.

Aud instantly recoils with terror.

AUD. Oh no! NO! Put them down! PUT THEM DOWN!

The Vikings gradually cease their mock battles and turn to look at Aud with incredulity.

ERIK. What's the matter?
AUD. PLEASE! You don't know what you're doing!
ERIK. What?
AUD. Put them down! (*To Erik.*) PLEASE make them put them down.
THORFINN. Why?
OTHERS. Yes, why?
AUD. *Why?*
ERIK. Yes.
AUD. But surely you know . . . ?
VIKINGS. Er . . . n . . . no . . .
ERIK. Know what?

Cut to a big close-up of King Arnulf.

KING ARNULF. The wonderful blessing under which we live here on Hy-Brasil!

The King beams. The Vikings shift uneasily. They look out of place and extremely scruffy in the midst of the scantily dressed courtiers of Hy-Brasil. Aud sits beside her father the King.

ERIK. No . . . we don't . . .

KING ARNULF. The Gods decreed that if ever sword spills human blood upon these shores, the whole of Hy-Brasil will sink beneath the waves.

King Arnulf beams rapturously at the Vikings, expecting them to be overjoyed. Instead they are horrified.

THORFINN. That's terrible!

ERIK. You mean if just *one person* gets killed?

KING ARNULF. Yes! (*He thinks: isn't it wonderful?*)

The Vikings look at each other, feeling they haven't quite understood.

THORFINN. You mean . . . you can't kill *anybody?*

KING ARNULF. Right! Isn't it wonderful?

The Vikings are non-plussed.

THORFINN. What? Not being able to kill anybody?

KING ARNULF (*bemused*). Well, of course.

ERIK (*interested*). How?

KING ARNULF (*explaining the obvious*). Well . . . for a start . . . er . . . there's no killing . . .

ERIK. Well, *obviously* there's no killing.

KING ARNULF. Well . . . [isn't it great?]

THORFINN. But how d'you take revenge?

KEITEL (*guiltily*). How do you punish people?

IVAR. How do you *defend* yourselves?

KING ARNULF (*getting a little irritated*). We don't have to. We're all terribly nice to each other. Aren't we?

COURT. Yes!

Aud catches Erik's eye and gives him a dangerously slow wink. A pause of disbelief from the Vikings.

SVEN. *All* the time?

KING ARNULF. Well, of course! We *have* to be.

He turns and conducts the courtiers, who chant in unison:

COURT. 'Being nice to each other is what it's all about.'
KING ARNULF (*rising as if to sing*). You see?

> We're terribly nice to each other
> We're friendly bold and free.
> We never say anything nasty
> 'Cause we dare not . . .

COURT (almost *singing*). No sirreeeee!

They hold the note while King Arnulf looks anxiously at the Vikings.

KING ARNULF. Would you like us to sing to you?
ERIK. That's very kind of you, but we're in rather a hurry . . .
We're . . .

King Arnulf claps and the court stop singing.

KING ARNULF. What's the matter, don't you *want* to hear our singing?
ERIK. Oh . . . well, yes, of course; it's just we're looking for the Horn Resounding and —
KING ARNULF. You don't think our singing's going to be good enough for you?
ERIK. Oh, no no no! It's just the Horn Resounding is . . .
KING ARNULF. A lot of people like our singing.
ERIK. I'm sure it's lovely.
KING ARNULF. But you don't want to hear it.
ERIK (*changing tack*). No . . . no . . . (*He looks at the others.*) We'd love to hear it. Wouldn't we?
VIKINGS. Oh . . . yes.
KING ARNULF. Well, you'll have to ask us *really* nicely.
ERIK (*realizing he has to be diplomatic*). Er . . . well . . . we . . . we . . . would be *terribly* grateful if you . . . all . . . would sing for us.
KING ARNULF. You're just saying that.
SVEN. Well, of course he is!

SVEN'S DAD. Sh!

They restrain Sven.

ERIK. Of course we're not; we'd genuinely like to hear you
sing.
KING ARNULF. *Really?*
ERIK. Really.
KING ARNULF. And you're not just saying it because you
think we want you to?

Erik swallows hard.

ERIK. No. (*He bites the lie.*)
KING ARNULF. Right! Summon the musicians! We'll do the
one that goes 'TUM-TUM-TUM-TUM-TI-TUM-TUM'.
COURT (*disappointed*). Oh . . . . . .
CHAMBERLAIN. *Really?*
KING ARNULF (*apologetically to Vikings*). It isn't the one we're
best at.
CHAMBERLAIN. Couldn't we do the one that goes 'TUM-TI-
TUM-TI-TUM-TI-TUM'?

The rest of the court look hopeful.

KING ARNULF (*whispering*). Not when we've got guests.
VOICE FROM COURT. How about the one that goes 'TI-TUM-
TI-TUM-TI-TUM-TI-TI-TUM'?
KING ARNULF. Don't be silly.
CHAMBERLAIN. That was a stupid suggestion.
VOICE. Sorry! I just thought they might like to hear something
that we can do.
ANOTHER. Yes! At least we know that one.
YET ANOTHER VOICE. Nobody knows the 'TUM-TUM-TUM-
TUM-TI-TUM-TUM' one.
REST OF COURT. No! Right! I agree!
ODD MAN OUT. I do!
REST OF COURT. Sh!
ANOTHER VOICE. It's too difficult!
CHAMBERLAIN. Sh!

KING ARNULF. All right. We'll do the one that goes 'TI-TUM-TI-TUM-TI-TUM-TI-TI-TUM'. Ah! The musicians!

The musicians are huge, unshaven, have broken noses and tattoos, and are covered in black oil – like mechanics. Their instruments are like heavy industrial machinery, pushed in large vats of black oil that drip all over the show.

KING ARNULF. Right . . . Oh dear . . . (*He glances across at the Vikings.*) I'm sure you're not going to like this . . .

Erik and the others smile reassuringly.
There is a lot of coughing. The King raises his baton and then brings it down, humming to himself as he does so. There is a most awful din: caterwauling, crashing and banging, whining, screaming . . .
The Vikings look at each other, trying to pick out some tune, but it's impossible.
Ivar the Boneless can't stop himself bursting out into giggles and this eventually spreads to the other Vikings. King Arnulf notices and bangs the throne for silence.
Gradually the din stops. King Arnulf sinks down in despair.

KING ARNULF (*tragically*). We're just not a very musical nation . . .

ERIK. No, no . . . It was very . . . er, nice.

KING ARNULF. Now I want you to be *absolutely*, totally, genuinely honest with me. Did you really, truly, honestly like it?

Erik thinks for some moments and then decides to make a clean breast of it.

ERIK. No.

KING ARNULF (*goes hysterical*). They didn't like it! Oh God! I want to die!

The whole court looks as if it's about to commit mass hara-kiri, while the musicians look rather dangerous.
Erik takes the moment to get down to business.

ERIK. Your Majesty! We come from a world where there *is* no music, where men live and die by the axe and by the sword . . .

KING ARNULF. Well, how d'you think *I* feel?

ERIK. The Gods are asleep, King Arnulf.

KING ARNULF. *You* try to be nice to people, when they're rude about your singing . . .

Erik feels he is making a mess of all this diplomacy.

ERIK. We must find the Horn Resounding!

The King glares at Erik.

ERIK. Is it *here* in Hy-Brasil?

King Arnulf thinks for a moment and then speaks.

KING ARNULF. I'll tell you what . . .

ERIK. Yes?

King Arnulf hesitates – he bites his lip and then takes the plunge.

KING ARNULF. We'll do the one that goes 'TUM-TUM-TUM-TUM-TI-TUM-TUM'. Perhaps you'll like that better.

Erik gives up.
A lot of throat clearing.
Aud, the King's daughter, gives Erik another dangerously slow wink.
The terrible 'music' starts up, shattering the calm of the beautiful city.
Fade.

Fade up on Golden Dragon *now afloat once more, riding at anchor in the bay. Ivar is standing on guard in it. Suddenly he sees something that makes him gape in horror.*
   We don't find out what it is, however, because we immediately

Cut to Erik. He is deeply in love. He is also in bed with the King's nubile daughter, Aud.

AUD. Have you ever felt like this about anyone else?

ERIK. What . . . you mean 'got into bed with' them?

AUD. No, of course not, silly – I mean *felt* like this about them?

ERIK. You mean . . . you *have* got into bed with somebody else?

AUD. No, I mean have you ever felt that for the first time in your life you'd met somebody you could believe in with your whole heart . . . someone whose goals suddenly seem to be *your* goals . . . whose dreams seem to be *your* dreams?

ERIK. *Have* you ever been to bed with anyone else?

AUD. What does that matter? But you've . . . you've . . . *felt* like this before . . .

ERIK. It was different . . .

AUD (*just for a moment it is Helga speaking*). What was she like?

ERIK. Oh . . . oh, I didn't know her very well . . .

AUD. But you *loved* her all the same . . .

ERIK. We never went to bed together.

AUD. Why do you go on about that? What does it matter?

ERIK. You've been to bed with somebody else, haven't you?

AUD. I've never *loved* anybody!

ERIK. *I've* never been to bed with anybody!

Suddenly there is a banging on the door.

KING ARNULF (v/o). Open up! I know you're in there!

AUD. Ah! It's my father!

KING ARNULF (v/o). Open up! I know you're in there!

Suddenly the note from Ivar's horn rings out across from the bay. Erik rushes to the window and looks out to see what Ivar saw previously: a black ship approaching on the horizon.

ERIK. Oh, no! Halfdan!

There is more banging on the bedroom door.

KING ARNULF (v/o). Aud! You've got someone in there again, haven't you?

Erik gives her a sharp look.

AUD. Quick! Throw this over you!

She throws a shabby bit of cloth over Erik and at that moment the door bursts open, and King Arnulf enters.

KING ARNULF. Right! Where is he?

AUD. Who, Father?

KING ARNULF. Who? Who? Whoever you've got in here of course!

AUD. There *is* no one.

The King starts prowling round the chamber. Erik stands there, naked and petrified, with the cloak hanging over his head, just where it landed.

KING ARNULF. I can *smell* one of those strangers . . . That's who it is, isn't it?

Aud keeps mum.

KING ARNULF. This is the fifth one this week.

Before he can stop himself, Erik blurts out:

ERIK. Fifth . . .

Aud motions him to be quiet, but it's too late. The King spins round to see who she is signalling to. The King appears to be looking straight at Erik. Erik can hardly bear the suspense.

KING ARNULF. Well . . . where is he?

AUD. There's nobody here, Father. Look for yourself.

King Arnulf looks round the chamber carefully. He looks straight through Erik as if he weren't there. Suddenly the King strides over to Erik and Erik instinctively cowers out of the way. The King walks straight over to a very small cupboard no more than a foot high, flings the door of it open, and starts throwing clothes around the room.

AUD. He wouldn't be a midget, Father!

The King turns on her.

KING ARNULF. Ah! So you admit there *is* someone!

AUD. You're losing your temper!

KING (*becoming instantly pleasant*). Of course I'm not. I never lose my temper . . .

Ivar's horn sounds again. A shadow passes over King Arnulf's face.

KING ARNULF. Oh dear . . . more visitors!

He strides to the window and sees Halfdan's ship. As he does so, Erik has to leap out of the way, inadvertently knocking a chest. The King spins round and addresses the chest.

KING ARNULF. Come out . . . Come out like a man . . . I know you're in there . . .

King Arnulf flings the chest open, revealing nothing but clothes. He is baffled. He reluctantly starts to leave.

AUD (*gently*). It's all in your own mind, Father . . . It's *you* who imagine that I'm always up here with some man or other . . .

KING ARNULF. I don't know how you do it, Aud . . . I sometimes think you've got some of your mother's magic . . .

He suddenly spies a small trinket-box and looks in that. But he doesn't find any strange man in it.

AUD. There is no magic, Father . . . My mother had no magic . . .

KING ARNULF. She did, I tell you! She could blind me as easily as the night the day.

AUD. It's your fantasy . . .

KING ARNULF. But one day I'll catch you . . . Like I caught her . . .

He leaves. Aud closes the door.
Erik throws the cloak off and starts getting dressed.

AUD. The Cloak Invisible. It was my mother's parting gift.

ERIK. 'The fifth one this week'!

AUD. Oh, for goodness' sake!

ERIK. And I thought you said it was something special . . .

Aud runs to his side and puts her arms around him.

AUD. That's just what I was trying to tell you. You *are* . . .

ERIK. Five this week; how many the week before?

AUD. You're as bad as my father.

ERIK. And the week before that?

AUD. Erik . . . ! (*She is really sincere.*) I want to help you get to Asgaard.

Erik is torn. He doesn't know whether to believe her or not. Ivar's horn sounds for a third time. Erik races to the window. He looks out. Halfdan's ship is even closer.

ERIK. We mustn't let him land!

AUD. Who?

ERIK. Halfdan the Black.

AUD. But, Erik . . .

But Erik is off out of the door.

AUD. No. Wait! My father will be —

There is a thump and a yell as Erik is set upon by the King's two musicians.

KING ARNULF. I might have known it was you!

MUSICIAN I (*pinning Erik's arms behind him*). I'm not hurting you, am I?

ERIK. What?

MUSICIAN 2. You *will* tell us if we hurt you?

They start to march Erik through the palace.

ERIK. Let me go!

Erik struggles.

KING ARNULF (*to musicians*). Careful! (*To Erik.*) They're not supposed to hurt you.

ERIK. You've got to let me go!

MUSICIAN 2. Oh no! We can hold onto you – just so long as we don't squeeze too hard or bump you.

In the distance we hear the horn again.

ERIK. Halfdan the Black's here!

They have reached a cell. The musicians start to chain Erik up.

KING ARNULF. It's all part of our safety regulations. You see if someone were to get hurt they might get angry and then . . . well . . .

ERIK. They'll be more than 'hurt' if Halfdan the Black lands! Ow!

MUSICIAN. Ooh! I'm terribly sorry.

KING ARNULF. Who is Halfdan the Black?

ERIK. He's trying to stop us waking the Gods.

KING ARNULF. Why?

ERIK. Because that's how he makes his money, by war and plunder!

KING ARNULF. Don't talk nonsense.

ERIK. He wants to kill *us*!

KING ARNULF. Not when we explain about the Great Blessing.

ERIK. You don't know Halfdan the Black.

KING ARNULF. I know that the Great Blessing has kept the peace for a thousand years, and will keep it for the next thousand.

The horn sounds again. Erik is about to argue this point when Thorfinn suddenly bursts in.

THORFINN. Erik!

MUSICIAN 2. We're not hurting him.

MUSICIAN 1 (*to Erik*). Are we?

ERIK. Just let me go!

THORFINN. Halfdan the Black's here!

ERIK. I know!

THORFINN (*to the King*). He wants to *kill* us.

They both look at King Arnulf. The King thinks.

ERIK. You don't want him to kill us *on* Hy-Brasil! Do you?

The King thinks some more. The horn sounds once more.

Cut to Golden Dragon. *Erik and the Vikings are scrambling into their war gear. They glance nervously over to where Halfdan the Black's ship is riding on the waves.*

THORFINN. I feel strange.

Erik looks round at Thorfinn, shocked.

IVAR THE BONELESS (*his throat dry*). Sort of wobbly and excited?
THORFINN. Sort of . . .
IVAR. That's fear.
SVEN. But Thorfinn doesn't know the meaning of fear.
THORFINN. Is it sort of . . . like a sinking feeling in your stomach?
IVAR. That's it!
ERIK. But. You're not even afraid of *death*, Thorfinn!
THORFINN. I know. I know.
SVEN'S DAD. It's magic.
ERIK. What 'magic'?
SVEN'S DAD. I've heard stories of a magic that strikes fear into the heart so you cannot fight.
SVEN (*deadly serious*). Yes . . . *I* can feel it.
IVAR THE BONELESS (*eagerly*). I always feel like this!

Suddenly Halfdan's ship rises up out of the water, and reveals the secret of its hidden power. Under the water-line is another line of oars! The Vikings are dumbfounded. Ivar drops trembling to his knees. The rest go white. Thorfinn draws his sword. Erik realizes his men are rapidly talking themselves into a blue funk.

ERIK. It's not magic! It's just a trick!
THORFINN (*turning on him angrily*). Don't you *feel* it?

Erik looks around at his paralysed crew. He realizes he is the only one who can save the situation.

ERIK. Very well! If they're using magic – we'll use magic of our own!

He leaps out of Golden Dragon *and races up to the shore towards the city of Hy-Brasil.*

Erik races into the Forum and gazes up at the high walls of the Palace. Without a thought he produces two daggers and plunges them into the stonework. Then he hauls himself up the sheer cliff of wall up to Aud's bedchamber fist over fist. It is, indeed, a prodigious feat. He arrives at Aud's window exhausted. Aud, who has appeared at the window, looks at him curiously.

AUD. Why didn't you come up by the stairs?

Erik looks around and notices for the first time the magnificent flights of stairs leading up to the top of Aud's tower.

ERIK (*rather miffed*). Just give me a hand.
AUD. I mean, you could have killed yourself.

Erik clambers into Aud's room.

ERIK. Where's the Cloak Invisible?
AUD. Why?

Erik looks around and is suddenly suspicious.

ERIK. I can't see it! (*Indignation suddenly seizes him.*) Have you got another man in here?

Erik starts feeling the air as if expecting to find an invisible body.

AUD. It's in the chest.

Erik races over and grabs the cloak.

AUD. No!
ERIK. I'll bring it back.
AUD. Erik. You don't understand.
ERIK. No. It's *you* who doesn't understand, Aud. Halfdan

has come to kill and destroy. We brought him here. We must stop him.

AUD (*pointing at the cloak*). But you don't realize . . .

ERIK. Goodbye, Aud . . .

Erik leaps out of the window.
For a moment Aud is surprised and then alarmed as she realizes he's jumped out of the window, which is some forty feet off the ground.

AUD. Erik!

She rushes to the window in time to see Erik parachuting down, holding the four corners of the cloak.

Erik lands safely and waves the cloak.

ERIK. And thanks for the Cloak Invisible!

AUD. No! WAIT! ERIK! The Cloak! The Cloak Invisible! It only seems to work on my father!

But Erik cannot hear her. He is already racing back to his ship.

Back on Golden Dragon, *Thorfinn is taking 'Being Scared' lessons from Ivar the Boneless.*

THORFINN. And a sort of slightly sick feeling?

IVAR. That's it! *And* you keep wanting to go to the lavatory.

THORFINN. Oh, yes! I hadn't noticed that!

SNORRI. Oh, shut up, you two. You're making us *all* nervous.

Erik leaps into Golden Dragon *brandishing the Cloak Invisible.*

ERIK. So Halfdan the Black's using magic, is he? Well, I have a magic to match his! (*He holds up the Cloak Invisible.*)

KEITEL. What is it?

SNORRI. A magic dishcloth.

ERIK. To the oars!

THORFINN. D'you think I've got time to go behind that bush?

Ivar starts to drum and the Vikings begin to row.
Golden Dragon *heads out of the harbour.*

Cut to Halfdan the Black flanked by his advisers, Gisli Oddsson and Eilif the Mongul.
He gives a nod and Eilif bangs his staff of office on the deck, as a signal for the galley slaves to speed up.
Down in the galley, the slave master (a diminutive Japanese) stalks down the decks lashing the sweat-streaked galley slaves and cursing them in incomprehensible Japanese.
Fortunately (or perhaps unfortunately) a translation appears in subtitles.

SLAVE-DRIVER (*subtitled*). Row! You incomprehensible, horizontal-eyed, Western trouser-wearers! Eurgh! You all look the same to me! How I despise your lack of subtlety and your joined-up writing! You, who have never committed ritual suicide in your lives!

SLAVE (*whispering to his neighbour*). You know, I don't think it would be so bad, if we knew what he was saying . . .

SLAVE-DRIVER. SILENCE! Unceremonious rice-pudding eaters! How I abominate your milk-drinking and your lack of ancestor-worship and your failure to eat your lunch out of little boxes!

Meanwhile the Vikings are growing increasingly uneasy as they row towards Halfdan.

SVEN'S DAD. What 'magic' have you brought, Erik?
ERIK. You'll see!

At this point, back on the Black Ship, Halfdan gives another nod and Eilif raps out yet another command with his staff. This time the prow of the Black Ship opens up like a pair of jaws.

The Vikings see it and panic.

IVAR THE BONELESS. I've done it!

THORFINN. Oh, yes . . . (*He has too!*)

Halfdan nods again and another order is rapped out.
This time a harpoon is fired from the prow. It thuds into
Golden Dragon *and two of Halfdan's dog-soldiers start to winch*
the line in.
The two ships are hauled closer and closer.

The Vikings panic even more.
Erik holds up the Cloak Invisible and grins round at his men,
knowing he is going to surprise them.

ERIK. Here! Here is the magic from the King's daughter!

Erik's men watch, half sceptical and half hopeful.
Erik enjoys the moment of suspense. Then he throws the Cloak
Invisible over his head and shoulders and grins round at his
men triumphantly, imagining he has vanished from their sight.

ERIK. There! I have become the wind!

The Vikings look at him, rather puzzled.
Only Harald seems to be impressed.

HARALD. How did he do that?
SVEN'S DAD. Do what?
HARALD. Vanish into thin air?
SVEN'S DAD. He hasn't.
HARALD. Well, where is he then?

Harald looks around. He is the only one who can't see Erik.

SVEN'S DAD. He's *there!*

At this point Halfdan's ship suddenly bites into the side of
Golden Dragon.
Erik leaps onto the side of Golden Dragon *and swings across*
onto Halfdan's ship.
The Vikings react to the horror of Halfdan's ship biting into
Golden Dragon *and to Erik's blithe leap onto the enemy boat.*
Erik lands on the deck of Halfdan's ship, and grins at the
ferocious skull-helmeted dog-soldiers.

ERIK. Ooh! Scary scary! Don't we look mean?

Two dog-soldiers look at each other, totally non-plussed.
Erik grimaces at Halfdan's men, and does a little pirouette to
show them all that he's invisible from every angle.

ERIK. You can't see me! But I can see you!

He breaks into a little dance.
Halfdan glares at his advisers.

HALFDAN. What's going on?

GISLI ODDSSON. That's Erik.

HALFDAN. Well, why isn't he scared of us?

Erik, meanwhile, approaches one of the dog-soldiers and
makes silly faces at him.

ERIK. Boo!

The dog-soldier topples overboard.
The galley slaves watch another dog-soldier fall into the hold
amongst them and lie there stunned. His sword falls onto the
deck between the slaves.
One of the slaves throws down his oar, and picks up the
dog-soldier's sword.
The slave-master suddenly appears. Once again he speaks
immaculate Japanese.

SLAVE-MASTER (*subtitled*). Hey! What's going on? Your
big-breasted women give me no pleasure with their
warmed-up fish and . . . Urgh!

The slave-master strides down the ship to flay the offending
slave, but another slave trips him up and in a twinkling of an
eye four others have leapt on the slave-master (despite their
chains) and are extracting his keys.

HALFDAN. What's the matter? Haven't you seen anyone fight
before?

DOG-SOLDIER I. No.

DOG-SOLDIER 2. They're usually too scared of us.

HALFDAN. *Kill* him!

1. Harald Missionary (17 years in the land of the Vikings and not a single convert) contemplates the conversion of Unn-the-Thrown-At.

2. Keitel Blacksmith offers Erik his services
- to the dismay of the womenfolk.

3. Freya tells Erik how he can wake the gods.

4. Loki, the Blacksmith's Assistant, points out to Keitel Blacksmith the advantages of Ragnarok to blacksmiths.

5. Halfdan the Black
- a man of business.

6. Loki
- the Blacksmith's
Assistant.

7. Loki betrays Erik's quest to Halfdan the Black.

8. Erik grapples with the Dragon of the North Sea.

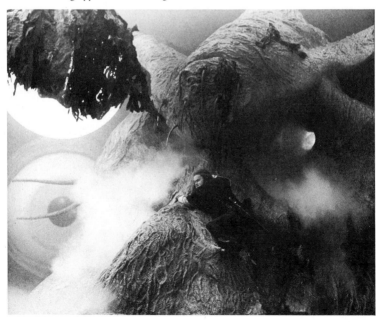

9. Sven the Berserk rescues Keitel Blacksmith during an unscheduled flight in Golden Dragon.

10. Erik and his men encounter their first Hy-Brasilian.

11. Erik discovers romance in the arms of Aud,
the King's daughter.

12. Arnulf, King of Hy-Brasil, fails to see Erik.

13. King Arnulf still can't see Erik. Aud keeps mum.

14. Erik returns to borrow the Cloak Invisible.

15. Wearing the Cloak Invisible, Erik takes on the dog soldiers.

16. Thorfinn Skull-Splitter enjoying a quiet moment of battle.

17. Erik finishes off the last dog soldier.

18. Rescued from the sinking of Hy-Brasil.

19. Aud shows Erik how to blow the Horn Resounding.

20. Sven's grandfather.

21. Aud gazes up at the gabled halls of Asgaard.

22. Erik and his men return to Ravensfjord only to find another threat awaits them.

Erik, still thinking he's invisible, is running amongst the dog-soldiers, having fun.
He runs one dog-soldier through and kicks another overboard, then he runs past a few more, right up to Halfdan himself. He whisks the Cloak Invisible off his head for an instant.

ERIK (*thinking he's revealing himself*). Here I am!

Then he turns and is off. Halfdan turns to his aides.

HALFDAN. What?

Back on Golden Dragon, *the Vikings' disbelief has turned to admiration.*

SVEN'S DAD. There! *That's* a true Berserk.
SVEN. I'm just building up to it, Dad.

Sven starts banging his head on the side of the boat.

SNORRI. He's gone batty!
THORFINN. No! The fear's gone!

Halfdan grabs a sword off one of his dead dog-soldiers and thrusts it into the unwilling hands of his military adviser, Eilif.

HALFDAN. Fight, damn you! Fight!

Cut back to Golden Dragon.
Now Sven leaps across onto Halfdan's ship followed by Ivar, yelling. Snorri looks back at Keitel.

SNORRI. Well! Come on!
KEITEL. I . . . I . . .

Keitel is thinking: 'Maybe I should let Halfdan win' but he knows he can't let a thing like that happen, now he is faced with the reality of it. The companionship of the voyage has brought them all too close for that.

KEITEL (*under his breath*). Hang the Blacksmith's Code!

Keitel leaps to his feet and joins in the attack.

Erik, meanwhile, is swinging across the deck from a rope.

ERIK. I am the air! I am the wind!

Keitel and Thorfinn are now fighting side by side.

THORFINN. This is the life, eh?

Keitel grins and strikes out.
*Ivar turns on Eilif who has reluctantly joined the fray. Maybe
he's singled Ivar out as the most harmless. Ivar suddenly
realizes he's only armed with drumsticks. Eiliff smiles evilly.*

IVAR. Ooh . . . er . . .

*Eilif's sword slices through Ivar's drumsticks. Ivar turns to
run, but is stopped by a dog-soldier. Eilif takes the opportunity
to run him through from behind.*

IVAR (*as he dies*). Ouch.

Erik sees Ivar's demise.

ERIK. Ivar!

*Erik leaps to take revenge. He jumps into the galley-pit and out
again à la Douglas Fairbanks in* The Thief of Baghdad *and
dispatches Eilif with a single thrust.*
Sven and his dad are fighting surrounded by dog-soldiers.

SVEN'S DAD. Well, go on! Go berserk!
SVEN. GIVE US A CHANCE, Dad!

Snorri appears from behind.

SNORRI (*to Sven's dad*). What about you? Why don't *you* go
berserk?
SVEN'S DAD. I got to keep my eye on *him* . . .

*Sven's dad looks uneasy. He is surrounded and, as a seasoned
campaigner, knows they haven't much chance.*
Halfdan smiles to himself. The battle is going his way.
*Thorfinn meanwhile is fighting two dog-soldiers but is attacked
from behind by a third.*

SVEN. Look out! Thorfinn!

But it is too late. Thorfinn is run through the back.
Sven goes berserk and kills all three dog-soldiers.
Sven's dad looks on, proud of his son for the first time. Maybe
their relationship will never be quite the same again.
Now Snorri suddenly sees something that cheers him up.
Slaves are coming up from below to join the battle. They are
armed with oars and swords. They join the fray, knocking
dog-soldiers overboard with their oars.
The dog-soldiers are suddenly outnumbered.
Halfdan's smile fades, and he looks around for an escape route.
The tide of battle has now turned dramatically as dog-soldier
after dog-soldier is tossed over the side or laid low by the
combination of Vikings and slaves.

Halfdan and Gisli slip into a lifeboat and sneak off. The rats are
leaving the sinking ship.

Back on the deck, all the dog-soldiers are dead or overboard. The
slaves and Vikings are cheering and embracing each other.
*   At the other end of the boat, Sven is cradling the dying Thorfinn*
in his arms. All around are jubilant slaves celebrating their
freedom.

SVEN. Thorfinn! You can't die!
THORFINN. I'm not frightened . . . of anything . . .
SVEN. You'll see my grandfather in Valhalla!
THORFINN (*dying*). No . . . he's not . . . not . . . there . . .
SVEN. Tell him I'm coming!

Thorfinn dies. Sven holds him and a tear comes down his face.
The danger has made comrades of the two rivals.
Erik, however, is still fighting a last lone dog-soldier; but just
as he is about to run him through the dog-soldier is stabbed in
the back. He sinks to the floor, revealing another dog-soldier.
Erik is outraged by this act of treachery and turns on the
assassin.

DOG-SOLDIER. No! No! Wait! Please wait, Erik!

The dog-soldier pulls his mask off to reveal he is, in fact, Loki. Erik is totally non-plussed.

ERIK. *Loki!* Where did *you* come from?

LOKI. Halfdan wanted to stop you waking the Gods . . . so . . . I disguised myself to sabotage their plans.

Erik has meanwhile been joined by the remaining comrades.

LOKI. To save *you*, Erik.

Erik is about to say 'But how can you see me? I'm wearing the Cloak Invisible.'

ERIK. But —

LOKI. It was my master Keitel's idea.

All eyes turn on Keitel who looks very uncomfortable.

LOKI. Wasn't it, Keitel?

KEITEL Well . . . I . . . I thought . . .

Keitel is overcome by the power of Loki's will, but he is deeply ashamed of his complicity in Loki's deeds.
Snorri gazes at Keitel with growing suspicion.

ERIK. But . . . How is it you can see me? (*He looks round.*) You can all see me?

LOKI. What d'you mean?

SNORRI AND OTHERS. Why shouldn't we see you?

HARALD. *I* can't see him?

ERIK. I'm wearing the Cloak Invisible . . .

Erik takes it off to demonstrate.

HARALD. Oh! There you are!

ERIK (*to the others*). You mean . . . you could see me all the time?

The Vikings look at each other, mystified.

SNORRI. Weren't we supposed to?

ERIK. Oh . . . I feel a little . . . oh . . .

Erik's knees give way and he faints onto the deck.

Cut to the King's Hall, some time later.

A victory celebration is in progress. It is a little bit like a Hampstead cocktail party, and the rough, battle-stained Vikings look rather out of place holding their little canapés.

Suddenly the King claps for silence.

KING ARNULF. We are grateful to you, Erik, and to your men . . .

COURT. Yes, we are . . .

KING ARNULF. And there is only *one* way we can repay you . . . Musicians!

King Arnulf claps his hands. Erik rushes over to him, anxious to avoid another Hy-Brasilian concert.

ERIK (*hurriedly*). Well, we'd love to hear you sing again, but what we'd really appreciate would be if you could see your way to lending . . . not giving of course . . . (*Continuing.*) . . . but just lending us the . . . um . . . the, well, to be quite blunt . . . the Horn Resounding.

All the time Erik is talking the doors of the hall behind are opening and a vast lur or horn is carried in by six bearers. One or two of the Vikings have turned to look and are now standing speechless.

King Arnulf beams at Erik.

KING ARNULF. It's yours.

Now Erik finally turns and looks at what everyone else is looking at.

Erik's jaw drops.

Everyone in the court beams at Erik, except Aud who is looking sad and disappointed.

ERIK (*when he can find his voice*). Is *that* it?

A cloud passes over King Arnulf's happy face.

KING ARNULF. Is there something the matter with it?

ERIK. Oh! No! no . . . of course not . . . it's just I hadn't expected it to be quite so big.

KING ARNULF. Well, it's not called the Horn Resounding for nothing. (*Aside.*) You *do* know how to play the horn, don't you?

ERIK. Yes . . . oh, yes . . .

KING ARNULF. Then I expect you'll be leaving first thing in the morning.

The King manhandles Erik away from his daughter. Perhaps we have the feeling that she isn't going to let Erik go as easily as that . . .

Mix through to later that night. The Vikings are lying asleep in the Great Hall, beside the Horn Resounding.

The camera closes in on Keitel. Suddenly a voice comes from the shadows:

VOICE (*whispering*). Keitel! Keitel Blacksmith!

Keitel opens his eyes and finds Loki close beside him.

LOKI. What's the matter, Keitel Blacksmith? Have you forgotten why you came on this voyage?

Keitel is silent.

LOKI. Are you going to let Erik wake the Gods?

KEITEL. How can we stop him now?

Loki looks around and then opens his hand in front of Keitel. In it is the mouthpiece from the Horn Resounding.

LOKI. Take this and throw it from the cliff heights. They'll never make the Horn Resounding sound without it.

Keitel frowns. Then an obvious thought limps across his muscular mind.

KEITEL. But why me? Why don't you do it?

Somebody stirs.

LOKI. Sh! Hurry!

KEITEL. *You* do it!

LOKI. You'll be able to throw it further than I could.

Keitel thinks. This is true.

LOKI. It must go far out to sea.

Loki presses the mouthpiece on Keitel. Keitel takes it, but reluctantly. Another Viking stirs.

LOKI. Surely you haven't forgotten your Blacksmith's Oath?

Keitel is about to reply and say he's been having second thoughts about it, but somehow he can't. Loki has such power over him.

KEITEL. I . . .

Suddenly another Viking stirs, and Loki hisses at him.

LOKI. Hurry!

Loki pretends to go back to sleep. Keitel (feeling a bit lumbered) thinks about his task and hesitates . . . Who knows? Perhaps he is about to stand firm, but Loki plays his trump card.

LOKI (*without opening his eyes*). Or I might have to tell Erik why you really came on this voyage.

Keitel is caught. He closes his eyes in resignation and then reluctantly starts to make his way out of the Hall.
As he gets to the doors he trips over Snorri, who wakes. The moothpiece falls a few feet away.

SNORRI. Who's that?

KEITEL. It's me. I'm just going to water the dragon . . . (*He gives a false laugh.*)

SNORRI. Oh . . .

Snorri notices the silver mouthpiece on the floor, but he pretends he hasn't.

SNORRI. Oh . . . clumsy idiot.

Snorri pretends to go back to sleep, but he opens one eye and watches Keitel Blacksmith recover the mouthpiece, and then follows Keitel out.
Loki gets up too. He follows to keep an eye on Snorri.

Cut to Aud on the shore, gazing moodily out to sea. She is brooding on Erik's imminent departure.
Suddenly a stone falls from above; she looks up and sees a figure appear on the cliff above. Hurriedly she withdraws into the shadows.
Keitel Blacksmith appears on the cliff-top. In his hands he holds the mouthpiece of the Horn Resounding. He examines it, turning over in his mind whether he is doing the right thing or not. Then he decides he must.

KEITEL (*to himself*). My fellow blacksmiths.

He prepares to throw it.

SNORRI. Keitel!

Keitel jumps out of his skin.

KEITEL. What?
SNORRI. What are you doing, Keitel Blacksmith?
KEITEL. Get away, Snorri.
SNORRI. What have you got there?

Snorri advances towards Keitel. Keitel backs away, danger-ously near to the edge of the cliff. His boot slips and he jerks himself forward. At the same time Snorri makes a grab for the mouthpiece.
A scuffle ensues, during which the mouthpiece of the Horn Resounding is dropped.
It bounces off the cliff and falls down to the shore below.
Aud steps out of the shadow and picks it up. She frowns and looks up, and then screams, as she sees the men fighting.

AUD. No!

But it is too late. Snorri goes white, gives a hideous gasp . . .

and sinks slowly to his knees – revealing Loki standing behind him with a bloody knife.

As Keitel and Loki watch Snorri die, a drop of blood from the knife falls to the ground. The moment it lands, there is a deep, subterranean groan, and the earth begins to tremble violently. Keitel and Loki look around in alarm.

KEITEL. Oh Gods! What have we done?

Back in the King's Hall, Sven, Sven's dad and Harald are wide awake, but for the moment paralysed, as bits of masonry crash around them.

The cheerful figure of King Arnulf appears at the top of a stairway. He raises his hands.

KING ARNULF. Stay calm! This is *not* happening.

The King then hurries out of a door at the top of the staircase.

SVEN'S DAD. What did he say?

ERIK. Look out!

The doors of the Great Hall burst open and a wall of water crashes through, knocking the Vikings off their feet.

There is little doubt that the whole of Hy-Brasil is sinking. We see a street go down, a statue sink and then we

Cut to a close-up of King Arnulf.

He is standing at the top of the Forum steps addressing a crowd of anxious citizens. They are keeping surprisingly good order considering they are already standing ankle-deep in water, and the whole town is rapidly sinking around them.

KING ARNULF. Now, I know what some of you must be thinking . . . the day has come . . . we're all going down, etc. etc. But let's get away from the fantasy and look at the FACTS.

FACT ONE   The threat of total destruction has kept the peace for one thousand years.

FACT TWO   The chances of it failing now are therefore one in three hundred and sixty-five thousand.

FACT THREE   . . .

By this time the water is up to people's knees, and several have crowded onto the lower steps to avoid getting wet.

KING ARNULF. FACT THREE Our safety regulations are the most rigorous in the world. We are all nice to each other, we never rub each other up the wrong way or contradict each other, do we?

CROWD. No.

Rumble. The buildings sink and masonry falls.

CITIZEN. We . . . er . . . do seem to be going down quite fast, Your Majesty – not trying to contradict you, course.

KING ARNULF. No, of course you're not, citizen. But let's stick to the facts. There has *never* been a safer, more certain way of keeping the peace. So whatever's happening, you can rest assured, Hy-Brasil is *not* sinking. Repeat, *not* sinking.

We cut away to an unfortunate Hy-Brasilian who looks out of a window to see if it's raining, but is immersed before he can find out.

The citizens in the Forum, however, are reassured by the King's words – even though they are now up to their waists in water.
One of them steps forward.

ANOTHER CITIZEN. May I just make a point in support of what King Arnulf's just said?

KING ARNULF. We'd be delighted – wouldn't we?

CITIZENS. Yes, we'd certainly like to hear what one of us has got to say . . .

Erik, Sven, Sven's dad and Harald struggle out of the Great Hall, carrying their belongings and the Horn Resounding, while the citizen is still speaking most articulately in support of the King. They are almost in a panic.

ERIK. What are you all doing?

CITIZEN AT THE BACK (*cheerfully*). It's all right. It's not happening.

ERIK (*urgently*). The place is sinking!

CITIZEN AT THE BACK. Yes . . . I thought it was too, but the King's just pointed out that it can't be.

CITIZEN (*still speaking in support of the King*). . . . and, of course, we mustn't forget King Arnulf's *excellent* eye for flower-arranging.

There is a smattering of applause. A few people pull their robes up out of the wet.
Erik leaps onto a wall and shouts to the crowd.

ERIK. Save yourselves! Hy-Brasil . . . is sinking.

There are a lot of knowing smiles amongst the citizens.

CITIZEN FROM MIDDLE. Look, you don't know our safety regulations.

KING ARNULF. It can't happen.

ERIK. But it *is*! Look!

KING ARNULF (*ignoring Erik*). The important thing is not to panic.

CITIZENS. Quite . . . yes . . . we understand . . .

KING ARNULF. I've already appointed the Chancellor as Chairman of a committee to find out exactly what *is* going on, and meantime I suggest we have a sing-song!

CITIZENS. Good idea!

ANOTHER. Can we do the one that goes 'TUM-TI-TUM-TI-TUM-TI-TUM'?

Erik looks around in despair.

Meanwhile in another street someone is struggling in the flood-water.

LOKI. I can't swim! I can't swim!

KEITEL. Relax!

LOKI. I'm drowning! Help!

Loki grabs Keitel round the neck.

KEITEL. Let go!

But Keitel is pulled under. He re-emerges spluttering.

KEITEL. Urrgh! Argh! Let go, you idiot!
LOKI. Help!
KEITEL. You'll drown us bo . . . !

But they go under again.
At this point Erik, Sven, Sven's dad and Harald swim round
the corner, pushing the Horn Resounding.
They see the figures disappearing under the water.

KEITEL. Help!
LOKI. Help!

Erik, Sven and Co. swim as fast as they can to rescue the
drowning pair. They struggle to overpower the panic-stricken
Loki, but he puts up a manic fight.
Unexpectedly, Harald Missionary suddenly unleashes a
vicious right hook and lays Loki out cold.
There is a moment's stunned silence that is not unmingled with
indignation.

SVEN (*with hurt surprise*). You hit him!
HARALD. Well, it's what you're supposed to do . . . isn't it?
SVEN'S DAD. Look!

They look up as Golden Dragon *sails around a corner of the*
street, piloted by Aud.
As the Vikings scramble aboard, the sounds of the 'sing-song'
reaching a particularly noisy and discordant climax attract
their attention.

Back in what was the Forum, a crowd of unconcerned-looking
citizens is sitting on the last roof and just coming to the end of
another appalling song.

CITIZENS. . . . Te . . . Tum!
KING. You know, I think we're getting better.
CITIZEN I (*with genuine interest*). How can you tell?
KING (*a bit stumped*). Er . . .
AUD. Father!

The King looks up.

KING ARNULF. It's all right! It isn't happening!

AUD. But, Father, it *is*!

ERIK. Get on board!

CITIZEN 2. No *thanks*!

CITIZEN 3. Who do you think *you* are?

CITIZEN 1. Panic-monger!

The roof is now sinking rapidly, though the citizens appear as unperturbed as ever.

CITIZEN. Leave us alone!

SVEN. Yeah. Leave 'em alone.

AUD. It's sinking! Hy-Brasil is sinking!

KING ARNULF. Well, my dear, I think you'll find it's all a question of what you want to believe in . . . I have slightly more experience of these matters than you . . .

Unfortunately, at this point, the entire gathering of citizens, the King and the Forum Temple disappear below the waves.

AUD. Father! (*Tears spring to her eyes.*)

Harald Missionary has put his arm around Aud in a fatherly way.

HARALD MISSIONARY. There, my child . . . it's at times like this that this book can be a great help . . .

Erik shoos him away.

HARALD MISSIONARY (*with his usual promptness*). Right!

Golden Dragon *spins alone in the wide ocean.*
Fade.

Fade up some time later. They are all gathered in front of the Horn Resounding.

ERIK (*to himself*). We must blow the first note . . . the note that will take us to Asgaard . . .

SVEN (*nervously and with awe in his voice*). Over the Edge of the World.

The other men look up at the Horn Resounding, and begin to feel a bit nervous.

ERIK. We are going where only the dead have been before . . .

Erik takes a deep breath and then puts his lips to the Horn Resounding. He blows. There is a splutter, and one or two of the Vikings titter amongst themselves.
He has another go. But again, all he produces is a pathetic spluttering.

SVEN (*not unkindly in his manner*). Uh! Here! Give it to me!

Sven pushes Erik aside.
Sven blows . . . he becomes redder and redder. But all he produces is a splutter. He gets a bit angry.

SVEN. Thor's blood!

Sven's dad looks heavenwards.

SVEN'S DAD. You're not using the right technique.

Sven's dad tries to take it over.

SVEN. No! I'm doing it!

They start to struggle.

SVEN (*getting angry*). You're always telling me . . . *telling* me!

Erik tries to separate them.

ERIK. Sven!

SVEN (*to his dad*). Let me do something for myself for a change!

Suddenly Aud comes forward.

AUD. No! Don't quarrel!

Sven and his dad stop fighting, surprised by the vehemence in her voice.

AUD. We'll never get where we want to go if we fight.

Aud crosses to the Horn and inserts the mouthpiece. Loki glances at Keitel. He hadn't bargained for this!

LOKI. Er . . . don't blow it! You never know *what* might happen . . .

AUD. It has not spoken for a thousand years . . . You must bring it to life with a kiss . . .

She puts her lips to the mouthpiece and just touches it with them . . . almost a kiss . . . then . . . very gently . . . she begins to blow . . . a soft . . . slight note can just be heard . . .

Aud takes her mouth away from the mouthpiece . . . and the soft note goes on . . . reverberating . . . A sweet note . . . a magic note . . . the Vikings stand stock-still, enchanted by the sound . . . and the sound all the time is getting louder and the Horn begins to vibrate with the note. As the volume increases the Golden Dragon *itself begins to reverberate with the sound. Rings of ripples begin to radiate out from the boat across the calm water.*

The note grows louder and louder, and the Vikings, who at first were laughing and cheering at Aud's success, begin to get rather alarmed.

Louder and louder gets the note and the Horn shakes and the boat vibrates. Things start to be shaken loose, and fall onto the deck. Ropes uncoil and run loose.

A heavy block suddenly crashes down to the deck, crowning Harald and laying him out flat.

Louder and louder grows the note, and the Vikings have to stop their ears for the pain. The water around the ship becomes more and more agitated.

And then another sound is heard. It is the thunder of water in the distance like a million distant waterfalls.

And suddenly they notice the sea is running like a river – all in one direction . . . sweeping the ship forward with incredible momentum.

In no time they are engulfed in a mist, still travelling at a rate of knots.

Almost at once a pointed rock looms out of the mist ahead of them.

Erik flings himself at the steering oar, and everyone is thrown about as the ship veers wildly and just misses the rock, only to see another looming up ahead of them. The ship veers again, as a third rock looms ahead.

This time Sven has grabbed a coil of rope, and as they pass the third rock, he throws it like a lasso over the rock.

Loki and Keitel leap to grab the rope just as the rope goes taut and the ship comes to a lurching stop, anchored by the rope, but still swaying and buffeted in the racing waters.

Those on board shout to each other, soaked to the skin. It is difficult to make out what they are shouting.

LOKI. Help!

AUD. What are you doing?

LOKI. What d'you think? Help! Somebody help us!

SVEN. Shut up!

LOKI (*pointing at Aud*). She wants to kill us!

KEITEL. She wants to take us over the Edge of the World!

AUD. You want to get to Asgaard, don't you?

LOKI. How do we know this is the way?

ERIK (*shouting*). We blew the Horn Resounding.

LOKI (*screaming and pointing an accusing finger at Aud*). She blew the Horn Resounding.

KEITEL (*shouting*). Don't you see, Erik! She wants revenge!

ERIK. What are you talking about?

LOKI (*to Keitel*). Shut up!

KEITEL. She knows it was our fault!

LOKI. Keep your mouth shut, Keitel!

KEITEL. No! It's *you*, Loki! I should never have listened to you!

Loki looks around desperately.

LOKI. You've lost your mind.

KEITEL. We came to stop you waking the Gods, Erik! But I didn't want anyone to get hurt!

LOKI. You fool!

Suddenly Loki produces his stiletto and leaps onto Keitel, stabbing at him.

LOKI. I should have got rid of you long ago!

KEITEL. Like you got rid of Snorri!

Erik tries to separate them.

AUD. No! No! We are in the spell of the Horn! Hatred will destroy us.

ERIK. That's right!

For a split second Erik is distracted. He looks across at Aud and for a moment he sees Freya standing there.

FREYA. Once you are in the spell of the Horn, hatred will destroy you . . .

Then it is Aud once more. But in that split second Loki has stabbed Erik.

ERIK. Arrgh!

Erik staggers back clutching his arm.
Keitel gives a roar of rage, and picks Loki up bodily and hurls him out of the boat into the maelstrom.
The other Vikings look on aghast. Keitel turns on them.

KEITEL. He killed Snorri! He caused the land of Hy-Brasil to sink! *She* knew!

AUD. I didn't know!

KEITEL. Now she wants to send us over the Edge of the World!

AUD. How else d'you think we're going to get to Asgaard?

The Vikings look at each other amidst the roaring waters and the thick spray. Erik holds his bleeding arm and looks at Aud. Should he trust her or not?
Suddenly he turns on the others.

ERIK (*shouting above the din*). Do *you* know the way to Asgaard, Keitel Blacksmith?

Keitel shakes his head.

ERIK. Do *you* know the way to Asgaard, Sven?

Sven shakes his head.

ERIK. There is only one road before us, and that leads over the Edge of the World.

Harald sits up as he returns to consciousness.

HARALD. There *is* no Edge of the World.

Sven's dad bonks him again.
Erik takes the rope and begins paying it out.
With grim faces the Vikings turn and face towards the roaring of the waters, as Erik edges the ship further into the mist.
The noise is deafening. It would be almost impossible to hear any voice above it.
The faces of the Vikings betray their fear as they find themselves emerging from out of the mist at the Edge of the World.
They gape as they find themselves confronted by a Waterfall of Seas – stretching on either side of them – as far as the eye can see – water falling and plunging over the lip of the world. And in front of them – the blue sky continues on down and down until it shades into blackness strewn with stars beneath their feet . . .
Sven, Sven's dad and Keitel edge to the prow and gasp.

AUD. No! Don't look over the Edge!

Erik lets out a little more rope, until the ship is protruding over the edge.
Sven, his dad and Keitel peer over the side, and stare down into the abyss. They gasp.
From above we see the prow of Golden Dragon *and the backs of the Vikings' heads in plain view against a backdrop of stars below them.*

ERIK. Let me see!

Aud holds him back.

AUD. No. Don't look . . . The abyss will suck away your strength.

ERIK. I *must* look! Keitel! Hold this!

*Erik turns to see Sven and Keitel trembling . . . They hold onto
the sides of the ship but their legs can barely support them.*

SVEN. There is nothing we can do . . .
SVEN'S DAD. Helpless . . .

Keitel starts to laugh.

KEITEL. Ha ha . . . I believed Loki . . . I believed I had a duty
to blacksmiths! Ha ha ha!

*Keitel laughs a little hysterically.
Aud turns urgently to Erik.*

AUD. *You* still want to get to Asgaard?
ERIK. Of course.
AUD. Do you believe I love you?
ERIK. I . . . but I . . .
AUD. You don't have to love me. Just: do you believe *I* love
you?
ERIK. Yes – I believe you do.
AUD. Then let go!

*Erik hesitates, then he decides to believe in Aud. He throws the
rope away.
At once the ship shoots off over the Edge of the World into
space . . .
Everything seems to slow down, as the longship drops down
and down . . . the ship twists slowly as it drops . . . round and
round.
The Vikings gaze about them in wonder, as they find their ship
is falling in silence amongst the stars.
Harald comes to once again.*

HARALD. I'm still seeing stars.

Keitel looks round at him.

KEITEL. We're *all* seeing stars.
HARALD. No! I was hit on the head.

The longship falls and falls through the star-strewn space until it softly lands in a white wilderness.

On the deck the Vikings are huddled up, covered with rime-frost.
   It seems as if they have been lying there half-frozen for some time. Perhaps the entire adventure has all been a dream, and they have been stuck in the Arctic pack-ice the whole time. The hallucinations of men near to death.
   Aud tries to wake Erik.

AUD. Don't sleep . . . wake . . . Look!

Erik opens his eyes and, for an instant, he sees Helga. He blinks and realizes it is Aud who is calling him back to consciousness.
Suddenly coloured lights begin to play on his face.

ERIK. Bi-Frost . . . The Rainbow Bridge.

Above them the Aurora Borealis stretches up, magnificent and awesome in the sky.
Erik makes his way through the other Vikings.

ERIK. Wake up!

The others slowly begin to rouse themselves from their icy slumber and sit up, awed by the sight.

KEITEL (*whispering*). Are we dead?
VIKINGS. The Rainbow Bridge.

They all peer up at the ever-changing colours of the Aurora Borealis, hanging in the sky above them like organ-pipes.
But something is happening. The lights begin to fade to reveal a magical city on a mountain.
The Vikings realize that this is journey's end . . . they have reached Asgaard . . . the City of the Gods.
The Vikings all catch their breaths and gaze in awe.

ERIK. Asgaard!
HARALD MISSIONARY. Where?
SVEN'S DAD. Up there, you fathead.

HARALD MISSIONARY. Up *where?*

Harald looks round quizzically at the others. It is clear that he can see nothing.

ERIK. Look! It's real.

Harald looks around at the others.

HARALD. Hallucinations are real.

It's no use; Harald can see nothing.
The Vikings, transfixed by the sight of their fabled home of the Gods, rise to their feet.
Aud whispers to Erik.

AUD. The second note.
ERIK. The second note to wake the Gods . . .

Erik kneels in front of the Horn.

AUD. Gently . . .

Erik blows . . . a soft gentle note . . . He takes his mouth away, and smiles at Aud. Once again the Horn starts to vibrate and the note gets louder . . . the ship starts to vibrate . . . louder and louder . . .
The whole landscape starts to vibrate . . . louder and louder grows the note until even the stars in the sky are vibrating and then a magical thing starts to happen . . . The note fades as one by one the shimmering stars start to fall out of the night sky . . . they fall like silver snow . . . until the ship . . . the Vikings . . . Asgaard . . . the whole landscape is covered in sparkling dust . . . then in the ensuing silence the first light begins to glow in the Halls of Asgaard . . . then another . . . and another . . . Erik stares as if bewitched and slowly begins to climb out of Golden Dragon *. . . but Aud tries to pull him back.*

AUD. Erik! You've done what you came to do!
ERIK. Not quite . . .

Aud looks at him.

AUD. Blow the third note! The note to take us home!

ERIK. There is something I must ask the Gods . . .

AUD. No living man has set foot in the Halls of Asgaard . . .
The Gods will never let you return.

*Erik looks at her . . . for a moment . . . But he knows he has
no choice.*

SVEN. I came to find my grandfather.

ERIK. I have to go . . .

AUD. Then I shall come too.

ERIK (*stares at her*). No . . . no . . .

AUD. I don't want to live *without* you.

ERIK. But, Aud . . . I . . . I came to find someone . . .

*Aud is about to say 'Her?', but she bites the word back and
looks down at the ground.*

ERIK. I'm sorry, Aud . . . I really am.

Aud kisses Erik, who then turns and climbs out of Golden
Dragon *and sets off across the ice.*
Sven follows.

SVEN'S DAD. Wait for me! I'll be dead soon anyway . . .

KEITEL. You can't go without me!

They follow. Even Harald Missionary starts to follow.

HARALD. Where are they all going?

AUD. Aren't you afraid?

HARALD. Oh . . . There's nothing for *me* to be afraid *of*.

Harald smiles and sets off after the others. Aud follows.
*The stars have fallen to form a shining, winding pathway up to
the City of the Gods. This is what the Vikings head for.*

Between them and the Citadel strange huge forms rise up.
*The Vikings approach and find the vast skeletons of the slain
giants. The Vikings are but tiny gnat-sized figures wending their
way between the vast figures.*

They climb the stairway-path of stars, up the winding road and eventually find themselves outside the massive doors of Asgaard.

ERIK. Valhalla . . .

Sven turns on Harald.

SVEN. There! It's real! It's solid! Now do you believe us?

He pats the wall of Valhalla – the Great Hall. Harald reaches out, but his hand goes right through the wall.

HARALD. There isn't anything.

Harald Missionary walks straight through the wall and disappears from sight.
The Vikings gasp, and run up to feel the point where he disappeared. The door is perfectly solid to them, and they jump out of their skins as Harald suddenly reappears again.

HARALD. You're having me on, aren't you?
ERIK. It's Valhalla – where the warriors slain in battle go.
AUD. It doesn't exist for him.
SVEN'S DAD. He's just a cynic.

At this moment there is a creak and the great doors mysteriously swing open.
As if mesmerized, the Vikings enter the Halls of Asgaard. The door slams behind them. They spin round, but the doors have vanished . . . No man has ever entered the Halls of Asgaard and left alive . . .
Erik slowly starts to cross the vast floor looking around him as he does so. One by one the other Vikings follow. After a while Erik stops.

ERIK. Listen!

The Vikings listen. They hear the sound of children laughing and shouting.
Erik and his men follow through the columns towards a pool of light. The scene that greets their eyes is not at all what they had been prepared for.

*Valhalla is not full of the warriors slain in battle, quaffing
mead on the ale-bench and reliving old battles – it is, instead,
full of children romping, laughing, shouting, quarrelling and
playing games . . . chess, fencing . . . dice . . . tag, etc.,
around a wide hearth fire.*

*Women are cooking and doing other housewifely things . . .
weaving, making bread, etc. It is a thoroughly domestic scene.
Suddenly one of them turns, and looks at Erik. It is Helga,
whom Erik accidentally killed in Scene One. She is once again
kneading dough. She has a red stain under her breast.*

HELGA. Oh good! It's Mr Wonderful!

Erik leaps to her side.

ERIK. I've come to take you back to the land of the living.
HELGA. What a stupid idea.
ERIK (*mortally hurt*). Why?
HELGA. What's the point of being dead in the land of the
living?
ERIK. I'll ask the Gods to give you life again!

*Helga looks at Erik very sceptically. She obviously thinks he
doesn't know what he's talking about. Aud reacts. Erik takes
Helga's hand – and gets covered in dough.*

HELGA. Have you tried asking the Gods for anything?
ERIK. Well . . . no . . .
HARALD MISSIONARY. Who is he talking to?
AUD. Sh!
HELGA. Odin!

*One of the children, throwing pennies against the wall, looks
round.*

CHILD ODIN. I'm busy.

The Vikings are recovering from their surprise.

VIKINGS. Odin?
HELGA (*getting back to her kneading*). He's busy.
ERIK. Is *that* Odin?

HELGA. You'll have to wait till he's finished his game.
ERIK (*shouts across*). Odin!

Odin leaves his game and saunters towards Erik.

ERIK. We have come from the world of Midgard . . .

The child whom Odin is playing with points his hammer at the ground near Erik and a lightning bolt zaps into it. Erik jumps out of the way.

CHILD-THOR. Clear off.
ODIN. No, wait, Thor.
ERIK. You must help us.
ODIN. We don't *have* to help anybody.
ERIK. Fenrir the Wolf covers the sun – men fight and kill each other the whole time.
ODIN. Why should *we* care?
ERIK. Because . . . you're . . . you're the Gods . . .
ODIN. So?
ERIK. Bring the Age of Ragnarok to an end and stop all this fighting and bloodshed.

Harald looks around at the Vikings in increasing desperation.

HARALD. This is ridiculous.
VIKINGS. Ssh!
HARALD. Right!

The other Child-Gods have stopped playing around now and are watching Erik and Odin.

ODIN. Erik the Viking! The things you seek are not in our power. We don't make men love each other or hate each other.
ERIK. But you're the Gods!
ODIN. Look . . . Erik . . .

Odin whistles. The other children look over their shoulders. From out of the darkness of the perimeter of the Hall, shadows emerge . . . shadows that, as they shuffle and stumble into the light, reveal themselves to be the heroes that the Vikings had expected to find in Valhalla. But they are not hale and hearty giants quaffing mead and reliving their great battles . . . they are, in fact, a sorry lot . . . the slain-in-battle still bearing the hideous deformities of their fatal wounds. Most have a sword or an axe buried in some part of their anatomy. One has been cleft in twain . . .

The Vikings react to this grisly gathering as more and more of them emerge from the shadows.

They gasp as they notice Snorri, Ivar, Thorfinn, Loki and Leif the Lucky.

ERIK. Snorri! Ivar!

HARALD. Here we are standing on a bare mountain top talking to thin air.

We notice that Harald's cloak is being blown about as if he were indeed on a bare mountain top. The others' cloaks are still.

Sven's dad is gazing across at one horribly mutilated specimen.

SVEN'S DAD. Dad!

KEITEL (*disbelievingly*). How can you tell?

SVEN'S DAD. I'll never forget him! The BASTARD!

Sven reacts.

Sven's dad starts to go berserk.

SVEN'S DAD. He drove me mad!

SVEN. Easy, Dad!

SVEN'S DAD. All his 'you'll never be a Berserk if you lose your temper' . . .

SVEN. Dad!

SVEN'S DAD. I hate you! I hate you!

Sven's dad collapses against Sven and Sven comforts him, understandingly.

A figure emerges from the throng of dead. It is Thorfinn. Sven looks up at him.

THORFINN: You won, Sven.

LOKI. What right have *you* to try and stop men fighting,

Erik the Viking? There is glory in battle. There are riches to be made and won . . .

KEITEL. Made by *you*, Loki!

LOKI. By *you* – Keitel Blacksmith! Don't you know, Erik, that is why he went with you? Ragnarok was good for his business . . .

KEITEL. It's not my business any more!

Suddenly there is a howl . . . a bitter howl that echoes above and around the Halls of Asgaard and that gets more distant and more distant. Everyone (including the dead heroes and the Gods) freezes and looks up, listening. Perhaps we cut away to the boiling sky as it resolves itself into the shape of a wolf that snarls and slinks away.
Odin turns to Erik as the howling recedes.

ODIN. Fenrir the Wolf has gone, Erik. But will men cease fighting each other? *That* is not in our power.

Odin starts to laugh. All the other children start to laugh . . . so do the dead heroes. Erik and his men look round uneasily.

ERIK. I have one more request before we return . . .

Erik turns towards Helga, who is still standing at her trough of dough with her arms up to her elbows in flour. Aud watches Erik with sadness in her heart.

ODIN. Return? You have set your foot in the Halls of Asgaard, Erik. You cannot return.

Aud looks round to see how the others react. It is as she had feared. Erik pales. The blood drains from the others' faces. Aud whispers something to Harald. Harald looks at her blankly.

AUD (*whispering*). Please!

HARALD. But you're all imagining this . . . whatever it is.

AUD (*earnestly*). You're the only one who can. *Please.*

Harald looks around at the dumbfounded Vikings. Then he shrugs and wanders off, disappearing through the closed doors of Valhalla.

ERIK. You mean . . . we must stay here forever?

As he says this Erik's eyes turn again towards Helga. He is clearly thinking at least there are compensations . . .
Odin, however, is laughing again.

ODIN. Stay *here*? Ha ha! This is Valhalla. This is reserved for those slain-in-battle.

HORRIBLY SLAIN WARRIOR (*grinning cheerfully*). Yeah! We're the *lucky* ones!

A HORRIBLY SLAIN FRIEND OF HIS. Yeah. It's much better than dying of old age.

The ghastly and dismembered dead warrirors all chortle no end at the dismay written on the faces of Erik and his men.
At the same time there is a grinding, winching sound. All those around the hearth-place fall back as a vast grating is winched up from out of the flames.
The Vikings look at each other.

ODIN. For *you* there is only the Pit of Hel!

As Odin says this there is a roaring sound and the flames and smoke are suddenly reversed and as the roaring increases the flames are sucked down altogether to reveal the black Pit of Hel itself.
And now the Pit is sucking the Vikings into it . . . their hair blows . . . they try to withstand the force that is drawing them towards the abyss . . .
The Gods look on in some amusement. But some of the dead are concerned.

SVEN'S GRANDFATHER. Son! My son!
SVEN'S DAD. Get lost!
SVEN. Dad! Grandfather!

Sven tries to reconcile his father and grandfather, but it's no use. He is sucked towards the Pit.

VIKINGS. Help!
ERIK (*to Helga*). I tried to save you!

HELGA. Why should you care?
ERIK. I don't know! I just did!

Erik can no longer withstand the force that is sucking him down to the Pit of Hel.
Suddenly, however, Snorri has leapt from the ranks of the dead. He grabs Erik and tries to stop him sliding towards the Pit of Hel. But it's no good.

ERIK. No! Let go, Snorri!
SNORRI. I've got you!
ERIK. You'll be sucked down too!
SNORRI. No! Arrgh!

Meanwhile, Ivar and Thorfinn and Leif the Lucky have also leapt forward to save their comrades.
They put up a fantastic struggle but remorselessly they are all sucked down.

VIKINGS. Aagh!

The Vikings clutch at the stone floor, their fingers trace blood as they try to cling on . . . but to no avail. The first are already toppling into the Pit.

VIKINGS. Noooh!
VIKINGS. Ah!

And the rest – including Aud – soon follow.

The mouth of the Pit of Hel, through which the Vikings are now tumbling higgledy-piggledy, is a round white disc set in the unutterable blackness of the pit. However, as the Vikings free-fall slowly towards camera, they are lit up by a faint, reddish glow from below. They are staring, wild-eyed and screaming as they fall.
As they fall, Erik manages to smash his axe into the side of the pit. Thorfinn grabs his leg and holds onto Sven. Leif clutches at Sven's belt. Sven's dad hangs onto Sven's foot. Ivar clutches Thorfinn's foot. Erik clutches Ivar's leg and Aud clutches Erik's.
They dangle like this for some seconds, and look

fearfully beneath them. There they can see the Infernal Regions of flame and molten lava . . . somehow suggesting the face of a huge and sinister creature. No wonder they're scared out of their wits.

Meanwhile, Odin and Thor appear at the top of the pit and look down with mild amusement. Thor casually points his hammer and a streak of lightning zaps Erik's axe. It instantly glows red hot. Erik screams.

Suddenly we hear a new sound – a long, high, sweet note.

AUD. Listen! LISTEN! The third note!

But it's no good. Erik has to let go of the red-hot axe. Everyone screams as they start to plunge down towards the Pit of Hel.

Cut to Golden Dragon.
Harald Missionary is blowing the Horn Resounding.

HARALD MISSIONARY (*to himself*). I want to go home . . . Oooh!

Suddenly Golden Dragon, the Horn Resounding and Harald Missionary shoot up into the air and disappear from sight.

Cut back to the Pit of Hel. The Vikings are looking down as they fall – they are still scared but gradually they start laughing . . . laughing as they fall down and down until they fall out of sight.
We are left with blackness and just the white disc of the mouth of the Pit of Hel above, until the disc changes magically into the moon.
There is a series of splashes.

The note begins to fade and the camera slowly pans down to reveal the Vikings all fallen into the duck pond back at Ravensfjord. They are laughing and whooping and splashing each other.

ERIK. I don't believe it . . . Ha ha ha! It brought us *home*!
LEIF. But who *blew* it?
IVAR. Oh! Who cares? We're *home*!
THORFINN. Mum! Dad!

SVEN. We're back!

Sven embraces his father and dances him around with joy.

ALL. Yo hoo! We're here! We're . . .

Suddenly the joy drains from their faces and they each gape in horror. What is it they see?
We cut to see that out of the huts the women and children and old men are emerging – but they are anything but happy. In fact they are all bound and gagged.
Behind them emerge the sinister figures of Halfdan the Black, Gisli and maybe half a dozen armed men.
Halfdan and his cronies no longer look sleek and self-assured. They are haggard and desperate. Their faces are streaked with dirt and sweat, and their clothes are torn and soiled. They have clearly been going through a lean time, since Ragnarok ended, and have descended on the village for revenge and for whatever plunder they can find. They have a few sackfuls of booty with them.
They herd the women, children and old men into a pathetic huddle in the middle of the village.
Halfdan is spitting evil and hatred.

HALFDAN. Throw down your weapons – or we shoot the children first.

Erik hesitates . . . The others look at him. What choice have they? Reluctantly, Erik throws his weapons into the pond. The others follow suit.
Halfdan watches. His men stand around him in a tight group with their backs to each other.

HALFDAN. Good . . . Good . . . Right, now we'll just shoot the children anyway . . .

Erik is paralysed. What can they do? Half Halfdan's men are aiming their crossbows at Erik and his comrades, and half are aiming at the women and children.
They raise the crossbows to shoot. Their fingers tighten on the triggers.
Suddenly there is a scream from above.

HARALD. Look out below!

Everyone looks up and, amazingly, out of the sky falls Golden
Dragon *and lands fair and square on top of Halfdan and his
gang, squashing them flat.*
Harald Missionary staggers blearily from the wreckage.

GRIMHILD HOUSEWIFE. Harald!

*She rushes to Harald, while the Vikings rush to release their
loved ones. Great celebrations all round.*

IVAR. Look!

They all turn and see the sun rising.
*The villagers gasp in wonder. They've never seen the sun
before.*

*Erik looks around and sees Thorfinn and Sven with their arms
round each other.*

*Aud looks up as Erik smiles at her and holds her to him.
Then they all turn and gaze at the spectacle of the sun returning
to the world.*